Tampa, FL 33610

How to Meet
In Homes

formally entitled:

How to Meet

Under the Headship of Jesus Christ

SeedSowers Publishing
P.O. Box 3317
Jacksonville, FL 32206
www.seedsowers.com

Library of Congress Cataloging-In-Publication Data
ISBN 0-940232-53-7
1. Religious 2. Non-Fiction

Without Church Buildings

100,000 churches in China which meet in homes

8,000 churches meeting exclusively in homes in Latin America

2,000 churches meeting in homes in Great Britain

500 in Australia

200 in New Zealand

In the United States?

Probably less than 200 firmly established churches deliberately meeting in homes wholly apart from church buildings.

The church meeting in homes in America is a new thought. But the house church also holds within it this promise of the greatest change ever in "church" in over 1700 years.

There is a radical revolution of vast proportions looming!

WHAT THIS BOOK IS ABOUT

God's people gathering—***not*** in a church building on Sunday, and then in homes during the week.

No!

Rather: this book is about churches which gather in homes, ***never*** in church buildings.

It is true that every church mentioned in the New Testament met in homes. But moving meetings into a house is ***not*** revolutionary enough. Changing geography is of little or no consequence. You are but carrying the old things from the building into living rooms.

This revolution must be far, far more radical than going from pew to sofa.

What else is this book about?

It is about meeting the needs of hungry-hearted Christians who simply cannot stand to go to church on Sunday anymore.

Read on!

THIS BOOK IS AN
INVITATION TO
REVOLUTION.
A revolution in spiritual
depth—and in the practice
of church life.

A REVOLUTION WHICH INCLUDES

A people no longer attending a Sunday morning church service.

The end of the present-day practice of the pastoral role.

Replacing the pastoral role? A return to the first-century practice of the itinerant church planter.

The return to the practice of a church planter also includes the ancient practice of the church planter's *departing* the church he raised up. He leaves it once that church has passed through a solid beginning. As he departs, the church planter leaves behind him a church that is lay-led.

Contents

Part I - How the Church is now

Part II - How the Church Used to be

Part III - Starting All Over, Totally New, From the Ground Up

Dedication

This book is dedicated to the Christians in Albania, as well as those in Hungary, Romania, the Czech Republic, Slovakia, Poland and Bulgaria. If I would add anyone else, it would be to all Christians who simply cannot bring themselves to continue "going to church" on Sunday morning and who are looking at the ekklesia as practiced, "first-century style."

Prologue

A case study of the wrong way to have the church

Albania.

The world's first and only atheist country had just opened to the outside world. It was August. We were among the very first outsiders to enter that country in nearly fifty years. As our plane touched down we saw armed soldiers covering the surrounding pastures. Machine gun nests greeted us as we stepped out.

This country of three million souls had not heard the word *God* spoken nor seen it in print for almost fifty years. No Moslems in Albania. No Catholics. No synagogues. No Hindus. No Protestants. No religion of any kind and no religious buildings of any kind. All had been torn down or converted to other uses. No religion—*none!* And no people coming in to this country for two generations.

But what has all this to do with a book about a revolution in the *practice* of church?

A great deal!

In the first months Albania opened to the rest of the world, hundreds of evangelical Christians from all over the western world flooded into Albania. Soon evangelism was everywhere. The para-church organizations led the way in the evangelism assault.

Their work seemed to be aimed at winning students and young people to Christ. The ekklesia was not in the forefront of the minds of any western Christians. Or so it appeared.

An authority on Albania estimated that all the combined Christian organizations in Albania had won an average of ninety people per day to Christ during that first year. (30,000 converts.)

Note that Albania is the very best situation we have ever had or ever will for missions, mission boards, denominations, and para-church organizations to measure their evangelistic efforts. Of those 30,000 Albanian converts (in the first year), how many of them are in some kind of church gathering? Here are the results of the way Westerners evangelize.

Two hundred!*

Of 30,000 recorded converts, 200 are in meetings.**

What has that to do with a revolution in our walk with Christ and our experience of ekklesia life?

This: The way those Albanians are meeting is sheer death! "Church," as introduced by western Christianity is as boring to Albanians as it is to us!

After 100 years of being implored not to import our culture, that is exactly what we are doing. We are Americanizing Christianity in Albania . . . just as we have in all the other countries on this planet! For over 200 years now, we have imposed our culture (and our way of meeting on Sunday morning) on others. Albania lays open the naked truth that we are not going to stop

---

** I will update this statistic each time this book is reprinted. At the end of eight years, missionary and para-church evangelism, and church planting—encompassing hundreds of workers and millions of dollars—and now a drive for church building!*

***It is now estimated that between 100,000 and a quarter of a million Albanians have been led to Christ!*

and that new converts do not like "going to church" any more than we do.

American missions, evangelists, etc., have destroyed all hope other lands have of ever *discovering* their own cultural expression of the church. *Their way* of meeting together is never explored. That is the problem we are creating.

We have a gigantic problem of our own right here in America—Christians here find "church" boring. And it is also a *cultural* problem. Yet we have given the Albanians this *American* way of meeting.

That is not exactly true. *The way we meet on Sunday here in America does **not** fit Americans **either**.*

The way Christians all over the world gather as "church" does not fit Albanian or American culture. The way we meet is as bad here as it is there! What we have on Sunday morning is a man-made invention that reflects no one's culture, and bores all men of all race, color, and culture.

What do we do in America? And in Albania? And everywhere we have taken the gospel? We peddle one awful way to meet.

What is our "way" of gathering? Chairs are set up in rows. There is a speaker's stand up front. There is a pastor who is directing *everything*. Nobody talks . . . except that one man. The people sing a few songs they are told to sing. There is a prayer. Then the pastor preaches. Finally everyone goes home. We meet like that in America. And in Albania . . . and everywhere evangelical Christianity has gone on this earth!

As a result, the Albanian Christians are already getting one of *your* habits . . . it is called the Sunday morning *thousand-yard stare*.

In Albania, more than anywhere else in all of Christian history, we could have started with a clean slate and introduced revolutionary change. We could have done it *right*! It turns out that we are terrible exporters. And we are exporting our worst possible product. Albania was a blank piece of paper. We had the greatest gospel opportunity in 2,000 years. Instead, what we have is a living, breathing laboratory of all the failures of modern Christianity. Albania rises up and screams to us the sterility of our entire *practice* of the Christian faith, especially our practice of "church." We have imparted to these innocent people our dull, boring, lifeless, functionless, Christian-killing, *Sunday morning church service.*

Plus all of our other rituals and religiosity.

Put it this way: How *we* meet from 11:00 to 12:00 on Sunday morning is an abysmal failure. It is also the greatest single destructive force now operating within our faith.

Nothing undermines and destroys the Christian faith as does the Sunday morning church service. Yet we dare export this disaster worldwide!

There is a better way! For America. For Albania. For all believers everywhere. There is a better way. There is something far, far better than the Sunday morning church service.

To Christian workers in Albania and all other countries we have ever entered, and to all of us in America who are in charge of "church": Abandon what you look to Albanian Christians! Abandon what a "church meeting" is here in America. *End* the 500-year-old Protestant practice of gathering. Gather, yes. But this 500-year-old worn-out, death-inducing way of gathering? No!

Sunday church, as practiced for the last 450 years, is an unmitigated disaster.

If you cannot do something revolutionary, radical

and new on the mission field, stay home! If you cannot see that Sunday church is becoming irrelevant to Christians, then get passed up in this new millennium!

Come home from the mission field and go to church one Sunday. Then, when you walk out—after you have shaken yourself of the thousand-yard stare—ask yourself, "Is this what Albania will look like twenty years from now?"

Unless there is a revolution, a revolution here in America, *and* there in Albania . . . yes!

This book is about that revolution. Here and everywhere!

To the layman who is bored to death from 11:00 to 12:00 on Sunday: You deserve better. You deserve a *revolution* in the way we meet here in America, just like Albania—and the rest of the world—deserves better than it is getting.

Those of you who are American and English missionaries serving in Albania, already you are talking of Bible schools, seminaries, Sunday schools, theological books, and Bible studies. Open your eyes. It does not matter what you bring to Albania; unless you abandon the way you meet in "Sunday church," Albanian Christianity is going to be dreadful. And dead.

So also all other places on this planet.

"Church" needs a radical revolution from the top down. A new—totally new—radical . . . revolutionary . . . *upheaval* in the practice of "church" for this new millennium. Otherwise "church" is going to be as irrelevant in America as Catholicism has become in Europe. (How irrelevant is that? A typical Catholic cathedral in a mega-city in France will consider itself lucky to have six attendees for Sunday church.)

Right now, in Albania, one can cheer because people are getting saved. But your children will live in the curse of the church traditions being imparted *today*. If you should ever visit eastern Europe, take in a Sunday morning Eastern Orthodox service. (It smells to high heaven of death. Death a thousand years dead.) *That* is what evangelical Christians way of meeting will appear someday!

The way Christians meet today can, and will, kill everything else we do. Nothing we do—*nothing*—is going to counteract or overcome the destruction caused by the present way we meet.

Nothing can be cured . . . no problems solved, nothing improved, nothing advanced . . . until we totally walk away from this pernicious Sunday ritual. Do anything in Christianity you wish. Try anything. Experience the greatest revival in Christian history. The Sunday church service will kill it in sight of three years!

This book proposes something radical to the extreme. It introduces a totally new way to meet. This is not about reform or adaptation. This is about absolutes; this is about *abolishment*. It means throwing out the way we meet, *in its entirety*.

Beginning with a whole new premise and with a totally different vantage point. Beginning in dimensions that conform to nothing American Christianity presently practices.

A revolutionary new way to meet.

The following story will help you understand why this book was written.

The story will help you understand why your church meetings are dead, and why Christian gatherings all over this planet are dead.

Why many Christians, multitudes of them, cannot stand "going to church" any more. And Christians—converted so well—*stop* going to church en masse. They number in the millions.

This tragedy is also working its destruction in one hundred thirty other nations where the gospel has been preached and *then* the Sunday church services have been introduced. Christians stop going to those gatherings. They always have, they always will! Christians have two choices: (1) not go to church or (2) be miserable when they do go!

Those brave souls who do "go to church" on Sunday cannot tell you what was said in the morning sermon, not even five minutes after leaving.

Fifty years from now, new nations opening to the gospel today are going to look just like churches in America and England. *Dead!*

The present church service will kill the very heart, spirit and power of *anything* else we do.

Go with me now to Albania when it had been open to the gospel less than a month. Experience some of the emotions I had. See what present church practice is doing there, and here, to all of us.

PART I

The Way The Church Is Now

*"While God waits for his church to be built of love,
Men bring stones."*

—Tagore

1

The Tragedy

It was afternoon. The place, a home somewhere in central Albania. We were meeting on the front porch.

Twenty-five adult Albanian believers were present. About twenty-three of them had been believers *less than* a month. Keep that in mind . . . *less* than a month. This was their fourth time ever to meet. It was on Sunday.

This was a land which—a few days before—had no word in its vocabulary for God. Innocence was never more innocent. Here was a porch full of believers, one-month-old in Christ, in a land that had been closed to *all* religions for two generations. No religious traditions existed, and no one present knew any religious traditions or had ever seen any.

What happened that afternoon provoked this book.

We had been having the noon meal together on the porch. *Everything* was utterly informal. Then came time for the "meeting" to begin. I was mortified at what happened. I had thought this would be an uncorrupted *Albania-style* meeting. Everything had been so informal, natural, fun-living and normal.

Suddenly the people leading these believers put the benches in neat rows . . . just like "church."

Rows! As in a church building! Only this was a porch on someone's house!

All sat down, all faces turned to the front.

The meeting began.

In my lifetime I have been in *thousands* of meetings exactly like this one. Identical. All over the world. No difference whatsoever. None! We could have been in the United States, England, Thailand, Germany, Egypt, or Africa. The meeting was the same as it is all over this planet!

In less than a month the Albanians had already accepted this ritual as *the way* Christians meet. Missions, missiology be damned, culture be damned, uniqueness be damned, opportunity to be different . . . to get it right just once, be damned, it was going to be the same in Albania as all the rest of this world!

Here in this dark land, on this porch, with these new converts . . . we had a Protestant/evangelical Sunday morning church service . . . exactly like the one at the First Baptist Church, Anytown, U.S.A! A service that duplicated 360,000 church services in North America and hundreds of thousands of other church services all over this planet!

In Albania, in America, everything gives way to the all-enveloping Sunday ritual. This death-evoking ritual is—and for 450 years has been—the sacred cow of Protestant Christianity.

There it was again! Making its entrance into Albania. *One* person announced *all* the songs. *We* sat. We sang on cue. We listened. We did as we were told. We did not function—we followed!

Those in charge did not dominate that meeting—they *were* the meeting. Twenty-five adults on three benches set in neat rows (fifteen children sitting on the floor) . . . sat . . . and listened, while the ghost of five centuries looked on!

Now, let me tell you of the very moment this book was born.

One of those Christian workers said, *"Let us pray."*

As those three words were uttered, all the children suddenly dropped down on their knees on that concrete floor. They did that so fast it was as though they had all been shot at once. Fifteen children hit the floor, on their knees. *All* of them pressed their two palms together, closed their eyes, stuck their hands under their chins and struck that famous Now-I-lay-me-down-to-sleep pose.

That is when this book was born.

Albanian culture, uniqueness, identity and social customs had been raped before my eyes . . . by Western Europeans and Americans!

Those people up front were not laymen. They were of the clergy stripe. Titled or titleless, they *were* of the cloth, and they had a ritual to give. That ritual, please note, is *clergy*-centered! They were doing the same thing all clerics do; they were drawing their significance from their position over God's people.

And true church life? An organic, native expression of the church? Such holy matters never had a chance.

At this rate an expression of body life will never ever be known in Albania.

Most foreign Christian workers in Albania—or anywhere else—rarely ever have even heard of such concepts as this book is presenting to you. Eventually, many of those precious twenty-five believers will stop coming back to those meetings. The tragedy lies here: They will not know *why!* They will not be able to articulate their feelings: their boredom, their utter disinterest in this boring ritual. They will not fully understand why they stopped, nor will the foreigners understand why it happened; consequently, this same tragedy, lived out before our eyes on that porch, will keep on being repeated in Albania. A 450-year-old routine that dulls the spiritual senses of the believer.

Oh, in ten years there will be a church building in that city, with 500 people attending every Sunday. But they will be sitting there like pillars of salt, attending only because they have been taught it is their religious duty!

Why will the meeting be dead?

The Protestant church sermon, pews, rows, pulpits and the paraphernalia of the ensuing ritual are *lifeless, boring* and *spiritually* killing! Vast multitudes of God's people—from one end of this planet to the other—will stop going to church, out of utter boredom! Millions have already. Millions more join their ranks every year!

Just as *hundreds of millions* of other Christians have stopped going to church, so also will this happen in Albania; and *none of the foreigners* will stop to see that *they* are the problem.

And if, perchance, this central problem were identified, the likelihood that anyone would really know *how* to change it is *very remote*. That has probably been true for the better part of 1700 years. The idea of annihilating and utterly revolutionizing all there is about how we meet together is a thought not yet thought! It is a revolution *not yet* born!

This which is called Sunday morning church is stealing all that evangelism does—either in America or Albania. Foreign or domestic. Imported or exported. Everywhere!

We have seen what we *are* doing in *Albania*. Now come with me to the domestic scene, to First Baptist Church in . . . well, in any city . . . but in this case, my hometown, Tyler, Texas. Let's see what the Sunday church service has already done in this country to over 350,000 churches. Assess the damage with me and see what we have done here in our own country as well as the rest of the world.

"Institutional Christianity has become clear on every concept, doctrine, insight, teaching and practice that the human mind can conceive.
They have only neglected two things:
Christ and the church."

2

The Sunday Morning Disaster

Years ago I sat, as millions of other Christians do every Sunday morning, in a Baptist pew. And like millions of other Southern Baptists we all sat there with the *thousand-yard stare.* Historically, how did we get here?

We were all wearing very uncomfortable clothes. Second, we were all sleepy. And we were all present in that big room for one reason only: because all during our life we were told we had to "go to church." That a church meeting was awful, that it was boring, that it was catatonic . . . never entered our minds. "Go to church" stood above all else.

Let us watch the ritual we follow every Sunday.

The organ plays a prelude. The choir comes in. We stand. We sing a song. We sit down. Then we sing another song. There is a prayer, then there are two more songs, another prayer, then comes the offering, then a special song by the choir. Then a sermon. *That,* dear reader, is a 450-year-old man-invented ritual. We Protestants have followed that same order, unchanged, for *over* 400 years! All of us, from one end of this planet to the other. Unchanged. Think about it.

Of course, none of us in the pews did anything.

That is, we did nothing on our own. We were puppets, and "the *order* of worship" was the puppetmaster that pulled our strings.

We all stood up—once—to sing! The rest of the time we sat in a near-catatonic stupor. If you think it was bad in that church, go with me to a church that begins its meeting with this liturgy:

Keep silence
Keep silence
Before Him
Let all the earth
Keep silence
Before Him!

For over 400 years we have gotten the hint. The 400-year-old message: Pew space-fillers do not function. They sit!

Later on, in my spiritual struggles, I made a desperate move. I got up and moved to the balcony! It was a vain effort to alleviate the excruciating agony of going to church. The balcony was an eye opener. It belonged to the teenagers. It was *their* territory. They were making paper planes up there and they sailed them! They talked, giggled, passed notes, and *bushed,** too.

At the time I sat in the balcony, I was a former pastor and was then an evangelist. Most of the time I was traveling, and it was in those travels that I learned that the Protestant ritual and the thousand-yard stare were not Southern Baptist exclusives. That boring church service was *everywhere* . . . in all kinds of churches all over the English-speaking world. Same ritual. Same death. Same boredom. Same thousand-yard stare.

Please note: That even includes charismatic churches!

---

* *Bushing: East Texas for "smooching" and "courting." That is, they kissed!*

And it includes those churches which have added "worship" to their meetings. The Sunday-morning plague is universal, be ye Pentecostal, Baptist, Presbyterian, or on the cutting edge of "the restoration of worship." It is still pews, all facing the same direction, a minister, sermons . . . and the thousand-yard stare.

There had to be a better way.

There *is*.

Well, dear reader, you have stayed for two chapters. Those two chapters have been about one subject: the curse of the Sunday morning Protestant service (1) in foreign lands and (2) in America.

Why do we subject ourselves to the brutality of the Sunday morning church service?

There is a reason. Let us find out.

"If the denomination, religious organization or movement you are in is over 100 years old, it is probably dead!"

—anonymous

3

Four Awful Ways to Meet

Throughout *all* of Christendom there are only four ways we meet. All are horrendous! We will begin with the *Protestant Ritual.*

I
THE AWFUL PROTESTANT WAY

Let me assume you are an American. Do you know that *you* have never experienced an organic expression of the church of Jesus Christ? When you walk into a church service on Sunday morning, pews, pulpit, etc., you are participating in a ritual the British brought to us back in the early 1600's! That ritual is just not *us.* We are not British.

Sunday church is a foreign import! Dumped on us by foreigners! Now we dump it on foreigners! In fact, in the last century we Americans have cursed over 100 nations with this ritual. We have evangelized the whole world with the Sunday morning Protestant ritual. That is nothing to brag about. Where did the British get this abominable ritual? From Geneva, Switzerland. John Calvin did it!!

The Protestant ritual is man-made. Man-contrived. A ritual which man concocted. An accident of church history. But today it is—you might say—more entrenched than the Bible. Maybe more entrenched in our lives than God. (You think not? Some so-called churches do not believe in the Bible, but they follow this ritual. And I've even heard of *Christian* atheists! Even *they* do not question this ritual.)

This "way" we Protestants meet started somewhere between 1538 and 1542, making it over 400 years old! It has remained unchanged for all those 400 years. It was boring when introduced. It is boring now. It will remain boring forever.

But let someone start a church. Here . . . or in foreign lands. The same life-defying way of meeting is *in every land on earth.* Protestants on all continents, of all races, of all cultures, *meet exactly the same way.* Now consider that this Sunday ritual is also *the* major reason people who get saved do not go on following the Lord! To go on propagating this ritual is . . . well, less than smart! Christians cannot stand sitting in those meetings and suffering Sunday death. So they quit!

Hear what the unchurched—but saved—are telling you. "If God is truly this boring, I can have a more fulfilling life on my own. Thanks for saving me from hell, but you can keep your idea of church and that abysmal Sunday service! "

God's people walk out of church buildings because of *induced boredom!* They also say good-bye to the ekklesia. And the ekklesia is the very center of God's heart! Not to mention the fact that it is wonderful!

But herein is the greatest tragedy for *all* of us . . . domestic or foreign: That pitiful, dead ritual, which supplanted the ekklesia, is *not* an organic expression of the Christian faith. Read that again!

That ritual was invented in Geneva, and even *in* Geneva that ritual was not an organic expression of the faith in that city. It moved from Geneva to

Scotland. When it got to Scotland . . . it was foreign to the Scots. When it spread to the English, it did not match the English. When that awful ritual got on a boat and came to America, landed and began cursing us here, it did not fit the American disposition or mentality. This pitiful ritual is not Albanian and does not fit Albanians! Nor any other ethnos on earth. Yet in every nation on earth this very life-killing ritual *defines* our faith. That pernicious ritual is proclaiming to the world: " *This* is Christianity."

"This is Christianity. Draw your view of the Christian faith from the *one* thing you see all of us doing . . . our Sunday ritual." That abysmal hour exemplifies our faith to the world.

Do you also realize you have never experienced how you would gather if left on your own with other saints? Do you know that *you* do not know how you would express yourself in such an organic meeting? Do you know that this Protestant ritual has suppressed your ever knowing the wonderful experiences of *organic* Christian meetings?

Just who is John Calvin to conform 500,000,000 Christians in over 130 nations to one gosh-awful ritual?

Did you realize this ritual is just not *you*?

Nor does it have even one Scriptural excuse for existing.

Most of all, there is a way to meet that reflects your culture, your disposition, your natural instinctiveness . . . *your* own native people?

That organic meeting is waiting to shout to the world: " *This* is what our faith is. We eagerly, joyfully invite you to see our faith expressed in the way we meet." The world will be awed. And the world will have to redefine their view of what Christianity means. The world will have to give up its image of

Christians and take a whole new, long look at our faith!

Even an American is entitled to his very own cultural expression of the church! That expression should differ from an Oriental, Zulu, Italian, Eskimo or Albanian way of meeting. But right now we are all stuck with just *one*. That one way of meeting fits none of us. It is man-made, dull, boring. Deadly. And ubiquitous!

This tragic ritual, now ingrained in our very bloodstream, pervades our faith and the world. Are you up for changing this?

Some dead meetings really are deader than other dead meetings.

Go to Bulgaria, Romania, Hungary, Czechoslovakia and Poland. There have been Protestant churches (and even *evangelical* churches) in these nations for over 200 years.

Those churches, which survived Communist interference, meet in a more ritualistic way than we do. Their meetings are *really* awful! This is the result of the legacy by British missionaries.

Dear eastern European Christians, give it up! Americans, give it up! Western Europe, give it up. Let it die. Better, let's kill it, lest *we* die!

I was in Romania just a few days after it opened its doors to outsiders, following forty years of isolation. I saw 32,000 people gather in a stadium in a Romanian city to hear the gospel. (All 32,000 of them stood when the ministers entered.) Some 6,000 people responded to the invitation.

What happened to those 6,000 people?

What if—by some unprecedented *miracle*—3,000 of them showed up for "church" next Sunday. Those 3,000 new believers would have taken one sniff of that dreadful Sunday morning ritual, in those dreadful church buildings, and *they would have never come back again.* Never!

And we criticize *them* for not following Christ? The fault is ours. If we do not abandon the Sunday church service, evangelism boils down to an exercise in futility! Evangelism is essentially a waste of time all over this planet if you compare (1) the numbers saved, (2) the time spent, (3) the money expended *and* (4) the number of souls who actually end up "going to church." The converts who get as far as number four are virtually nonexistent. It will stay that way, forever, until we rid ourselves of that thing we subject God's people to every Sunday morning!

Theoretically, there should be thousands of new converts gathering in that city. Yet, if I were a new convert in Romania, I would *not* be attending a church meeting in a church building anywhere.

MORE IS NEEDED

Listen world: We will not have gone far enough if we only abandon the baggage of how Christians presently meet. There must also come a commitment in every nation on this earth to *find out* how each respective nation *uniquely* and *organically* expresses the church of Jesus Christ.

We all have a job to do, in every culture, land and tongue . . . for each of us to discover for ourselves *how to meet!*

Just how would we meet if we had never been to, never even seen, a "Sunday church service?" Give that question much consideration, for it is one of the most exciting questions ever put to a believer.

And how would we meet if we had never seen nor heard of a church building?

The way we evangelicals meet: Awful. Boring.

Utterly without Scriptural basis. Unchanged in over four centuries. Meeting exactly the same way throughout this entire planet.

But there are even *worse* meetings than ours.

II
FIFTEEN HUNDRED YEARS OF CATHOLIC MEETINGS

A gentleman named Gregory the Great sat down one day and wrote out a way for the church to meet. The year? About 540 A.D.. And for 1500 years that pope's Sunday ritual has *never* changed . . . not *one* word.

That pseudo-pagan ritual he invented that day was imposed on all Christians, everywhere on this planet, for a thousand years! Like it or not. It was man-invented, imposed from the top down.

Calvin only gave us slight relief when replacing it with the Protestant ritual.

We want something that has *not* been allowed us for 1700 years. We want the right to *discover* the *natural* way we would meet if all you ritualists had left us alone. There is a better way than Gregory or Calvin.

But even Gregory did not invent the worst way of meeting. That horror belongs to

III
THE EASTERN ORTHODOX

The most dreadful of all meetings was thought up by the Eastern Orthodox Church. It is a two-hour ritual depicting who knows what. (Yes, some do know the meaning of this incarnate dirge.) The Eastern Orthodox Church claims they got their ritual from second and third-century Christians. They did not, but do not tell them that, because they get terribly upset if you do.

What makes their way to meet the all-time horror story?

There is no place to sit down!

You have to stand on your feet for the entire, merciless meeting. No benches or pews. You stand. For around 1700 years now, *you stand!* And the Eastern Orthodox church wonders why it has never been popular?! They could have been a little less popular if they had served cyanide for the Host!

Now we come to another dreary meeting, not as well-known, yet fanatically held to, and—unfortunately—*extremely* influential despite the fact it is not a well-known way of meeting.

IV
THE "BRETHREN" WAY OF MEETING

The one I find the hardest to attend is the Plymouth Brethren type of meeting. The reason is simple. I actually know what is going on, and it is a heartbreaker. It *is* a ritual, and it is as boring as the other three.

Man-invented, inorganic, and imposed on God's people from the top down, yet called "New Testament." You see, the Protestants and Catholics never think about their ritual . . . neither to defend nor to promulgate; it is just always there. The Brethren-type meeting is zealously defended, protected and insisted upon. It also rivals the other three ways of meeting in its boredom. But its greatest tragedy lies in the fact they insist it is *the* Scriptural way to meet!

The Plymouth Brethren invented their way to meet in about1840. It is identically observed in *every* land, nation, tongue and culture. Go to one Plymouth Brethren gathering anywhere in the world, regardless of race, tongue or culture, and you have been to them *all.* Like the other three ways to meet, it changes not!

Vocabulary is everything with Brethren. For instance, most Plymouth Brethren churches have no pastor, but they have something that sure looks like one. They have no ritual, but their meetings are exactly the same every week. They are not a movement or a denomination, though they look *exactly* like one. They are open to *all* Christians . . . as long as you believe as they do. *And* they have chairs neatly lined up in rows! And a pulpit (a speaker stand) and "ministry." It all adds up to about the same thing as the Protestant meeting, except it is worse! Try it for yourself!

Catholic, Protestant, and Brethren . . . each has a single, *worldwide* way to meet. That is terrible, denying all of us variety of expression, and preventing the discovery of cultural expressions among the Lord's people.

If you are unfamiliar with a Brethren meeting, it has the following characteristics. (You have to cultivate a taste for it. Many non-Plymouth Brethren groups follow this same general format. Maybe your church does, and is not aware of it.)

One of the most obvious aspects of Brethren-type meetings is the observance of the "Lord's table" *every* Sunday. The *same* meeting, the same way! *Every* week, forever.

As A. W. Tozer said of another Brethren teaching: "There is not one shred of evidence in the New Testament for such a teaching."

The Brethren searched the New Testament* and—using the clip-and-paste, patch-quilt, jigsaw method of Scripture study, tying verses and verse fragments together—they came up with this "New Testament way to meet." But, boy, did they leave out a lot of verses they did not like!

Actually John Darby searched the New Testament, patching together disjointed verses from all over and then came up with "a Biblical way to meet."

You might enjoy this service the first two or three times. You might be able to bear the next ten. But it is an hour of unhappiness. Essentially, their Lord's supper meeting is a funeral dirge. Most of all, it is man-made; and like the other three ways to meet, it is imposed on God's people from the top down; it did not come into existence organically, from the grass roots *up!* But if you need something you can remotely justify as New Testament, dive in. It is not, but it flies that flag.

I have a notion that a thousand years from now (if the Lord does not come back before then), the Brethren will be holding this same meeting, telling Christians this is the way believers in the first century took "the Lord's table." Again, regardless of nation, regardless of culture, any place you go on this planet, this meeting will be identical.

There is *nothing* organic about Brethrenistic meetings; there is no cultural experience in them that fits a people comfortably, nothing to identify as "ours."

Why is it so dull and ritualistic? Perhaps because a former Episcopalian minister invented the thing! And, like all of John Darby's teachings, it reflects a secularistic, fatalistic philosophy about it.

Another attribute of the Brethren-type meeting is this: *Usually* women cannot speak in the meetings. At the least, in all gatherings influenced by Brethrenism, the women hold an *inferior* position in the church.*

Other trappings of Brethren type meetings:

Extreme emphasis on the Bible that virtually negates an indwelling Lord and a living relationship to Christ. Someone called this approach to Scripture and to Christ: revisionistic secular fatalistic philosophic theology! These teachings are also strong on

To "In Christ there is neither male nor female," they reply: "In Christ there is no male or female; but in the* ***church* *there is."*

conformity. The teachings imply "we are the overcomers." In them are also strong insistence on women's head covering.

CHANGE ANYONE?

There is an outside chance the Catholics will some day give up the Sunday morning church service that Gregory gave them. There is hope, prayer and dreams that some day we Protestants will abandon what John Calvin bequeathed to us. But the chances for the Brethren-type churches to abandon "the Lord's table" ritual is probably just to the left of zero.

WHAT DO ALL FOUR MEETINGS HAVE IN COMMON?

What do these four ways to meet have in common? Well, they were all man-made. Contrived!

Secondly, they came to us from the top down. A clergy at the top imposed these kinds of meetings on us. The way to meet did *not* come from the Lord's people . . . from the grass roots. *You* had a method imposed on you. You did not get to discover, in *your* culture, your social context, your matrix . . . how to meet!

There is a better way than all four! The body of Christ discovering for itself . . . *how to gather.*

It cannot be done? That is like telling an eagle it cannot fly. I have seen eagles fly! I have watched God's people birth an organic expression of the ekklesia. I have watched them discover for themselves that something they had laid hold of was originating from the bottom up! *Grass roots* meetings!

THE PROBLEM OF HAVING "NEW TESTAMENT MEETINGS"

You may ask, "Why not New Testament Meetings?" Well, there are two ways to look at the New Testament.

(1) As some kind of grand rule book: to discover—by rearranging verses together—how to meet, and then to recreate that way of meeting. (A grave robber-scientist named Dr. Frankenstein had basically the same approach to creating life. A leg here, a hand there, sew them together and voilá . . . a man! Somehow both manage to miss the mark.)

(2) The second way is to see the dynamic, fluid story of the first-century believers. You discover—as you see the entire panorama of their drama—that each and every ekklesia is *discovering*, for itself, *how to meet.* The dynamics of a Christ-centered gospel, the power of that gospel resonating in them, they—helped by their *itinerant* church planter and by an indwelling Lord—discover their own, unique way to meet. What unfolds, when you look at Scripture in this way, is an organic expression of the bride of Christ, unique to each city, unique to each culture.

Take your choice. One of these two alternatives is living, adaptable, fluid, natural, flexible, attractive, authentic, and a perfect statement to the world of what "Christian" is.

The other is . . . to be kind . . . the opposite of all that.

We are going to take a head-on look at how the discovery of meeting together took place in the first century, *and* how that discovery is happening today.

A revolution is needed. Radical revolution, on a dozen different levels, *if* a totally new way of "church" is to come to this earth.

We have a disease. It's fatal. It's called "going to church." The cure? Let's see!

We Meet Together the Wrong Way!

Why have we not addressed the central issue . . . that church services are horrific?

Having discussed that question with dozens of Christian leaders, I will tell you this: Men are terrified to address the issue of radically changing the way we evangelicals "do" church!

The reasons we have not faced this central issue are fairly obvious: (1)changing the practices of Christendom, or (2) changing the traditions of just one denomination, or (3) even changing one local church from its present ritual . . . the very idea would scare off a Martin Luther . . . or anyone else who would even momentarily entertain the idea.

Adapt, yes. Redirect, yes. Add on, yes. Overlap, yes. But start over, from the ground up, abolishing everything?

No way! The very idea would strike fear in Zorro, Batman, Superman, Captain Courageous and . . . well, you get the picture.

Now, dear reader, let us dare to do the unthinkable; let us consider a change in the way we meet that is every bit that radical. Let us consider a revolution of the highest order.

One that sweeps away all of the past. Utterly!

"We like the old wine better."

—Luke 5:39

"In their own generation they are known as revolutionaries, radicals, rebels and heretics who are ignorant, arrogant, proud, troublemakers.
They are known as visionaries, apostles and saints in the next generation.
But in both cases their words are ignored."

4

It Will Take a Revolution

The Sunday church service will kill new converts. Sometimes it takes six months to kill a people, sometimes it takes twenty years.

The cure? The cure is far worse than the disease! Any attempt at a true cure would split virtually any church.

For a people to discover for themselves how to meet will take returning to a long-forgotten style. It is the only way, but, boy, is it radical these days. Only the daring should even consider it. Here, stick your toe in the water and see how it feels.

The first thing you will have to do is abandon the present way you meet.

Step two: Start all over again. But that includes giving up (1) the centrality of the sermon, (2) the use of a church building, and (3) the present-day practice of the pastor.

Dare you read on? Well, this is not an add-on idea. We are addressing virtually total abolition of *all* that is presently practiced!

Who wants to do anything which is anywhere near *that* revolutionary?

Do you already have an established way of doing

things? If so, your way of meeting was established at the very outset of your church's birth.

If you dare try the radical way of "*lay* discovery," then you will have to abandon your entire past. You have to burn your *old* beginning. This is not wise. In fact, it is probably impossible!

Beginnings are always *all* important, but never so much as here. My experience says you *must* begin in virgin soil!! To break that lifelong tradition of meeting the wrong way is impossible. A new way to meet has to be part of a church's *very beginning.*

It is virtually impossible to make a major change in the direction of a group of people once a beginning has been made.

As you will see in Part Two of this book, the secret is in a whole new beginning. Beginning with a whole new way of church practices. Beginning with a totally different purpose than that which birthed past churches. The beginning is everything. That was true in the first century, that is true now.

How do churches start?

CENTURY TWENTY-ONE *MUST* GET BACK TO THIS MAN

THE SECRET OF THE FIRST-CENTURY EKKLESIA

In Century One, churches were all raised up by someone called a *church planter.* This crazy man (example: Paul) had a totally different approach to beginning a church. He had the idea that he would stay with them a short period of time, and then walk out and leave them. Furthermore, the Lord's people actually understood this and even thought it was a great idea! They knew that finding the *way to meet* would fall to *them.* To them alone, and *nobody* else!!

Back in those ancient days an organic expression of church life came with a church's very birth. (Surely we would never call the Sunday morning Protestant church service *organic.*) All they knew of church came out of the soil of survival. All we know of church came straight out of the Reformation.

Calvin and Luther gave us our present-day church practices. Actually, they *imposed* these practices. It was a political/military imposition. But back in the first century era God's people found their own way.

First-century believers explored their way into church life. Three hundred years later it was taken from them by an emperor . . . and the organic was replaced by man-made ritual. During the Reformation we came up with new man-made rituals. That we still practice them is an anachronism. To call the way we meet outdated is being kind to the word *outdated.*

Yet, no one has suggested a new adventure into discovery!

HOW REFORMATION "CHURCH" COVERED THE GLOBE

That brings us to you!

To replace this mess, will you venture into waters that have not been sailed on for 1700 years? Dare you consider *discovery*?! Discovery of matters lost so long ago!

Are you up to a change? A break with the very way of expression of church as known all over the world?

This is asking people to give up their present identity! Make no mistake, the way Christians meet together is the center and soul of *who we are.* Take that away and we lose our identity. How we meet on Sunday is the *one* factor that identifies us . . . to ourselves and to the world. Changing the way we meet means changing all the encompassing elements of identity. That, dear reader, is revolution.

Few tread the path of revolution.

But if we do not change?

Christians should gather. It is instinctive to our species. Yet, the way we gather *kills* that very instinct . . . and makes us not want to even think about something as awful as *going to a gathering of the church!* We are forever stuck with a short-circuit that nullifies the very nature of our faith.

The best thing on earth American Christians could do for the rest of the Christians on this planet is to stop our way of meeting.

That brings us back to that word "beginning."

A RADICAL NEW PREMISE

If you are to enter this venture correctly, you most certainly have to do it at the inception of a church. We *begin* with a whole new premise of the ekklesia: We move toward *Jesus Christ being the center of the ekklesia.* We move toward the organic. We get there by means of a hair-raising adventure!

The most significant point: The church must be raised up in such a way that the people are allowed to *find for themselves* their own way of meeting. How can laymen who have been silent for 1700 years discover an expression of gathering that is natural to their personality and culture?

It will not be easy.

Nonetheless, the church belongs to Jesus Christ and to the saints. It does not belong to preachers, clergy or ministers, nor is the pulpit ministry the center of the meeting. The focal point lies elsewhere.

There is a *different* way to meet for every race, every nation, every culture and every tongue. Each culture meets in a way distinct from the others. How to meet is a way to be *found, not* imposed. It is an adventure on a sea few have dared to sail. That adventure is high in drama and fraught with dangers!

For any soul in our day it is, at best, a long shot. A gamble. But it is exciting and life changing. At all costs, that *way* must begin to be discovered . . . again.

What is it that must end? Right now all churches have their beginning shrouded in an artificial way of meeting, imposed from *Day One.* The way that protestant churches get started, *that* is the first thing which must end.

THE INSTINCT OF THE CHRISTIAN SPECIES

It is native to our particular species (the new creation) to meet in fellowship, in great informality, in caring, in loving, in sharing, in talking to one another. It is native to our species to want to hear about the Lord Jesus Christ . . . *from one another.* (Not about ten thousand things that are *related to Him* but which are in no way really *His person.*) It is native to our species to have endless variety when we meet. It is native to our species, once these wonderful ways become a reality to us, to commit ourselves to one another for all the rest of our lives. It is also natural to our species to have an almost uncontrollable urge to get to such meetings. You cannot keep us away! And once there, we function!

But here is the most exciting part. It is also natural to our species to recognize an organic meeting when we see it. For instance, an organic meeting in China might look really unusual in America. Counterwise, a meeting that fits our culture might look rather strange to someone who lived in inland China.

This is as it should be!

In every nation we need that new way to meet. It is a way which is instinctive and natural to believers within each specific culture. The only way for any group of Christians to learn their natural way to meet together is to *discover* that way. *That* goal of discovering their own unique way of meeting has to be present at the very beginning. Everyone present must know that they are on an adventure, from day one!

Every person involved needs to know that in a few months they are, as a group, going to be left to fend for themselves.

> The first motion lies with someone who is utterly foreign to your understanding. He is called an itinerant church planter. It is the responsibility of the church planter to so order his life and his work, and to so lead God's people, that *they*—not he—make the discovery of *how to meet.* Not only how to meet, but how to behave, function, express themselves, and most of all . . . how to care for and love one another. This will be done, and after these helps and directions are shared, the church planter walks out on them . . . leaving them leaderless!
>
> Is that Scriptural? Well, read Part Two and see for yourself. What emerges will be new for you and it will be different in every land. That expression will even vary a bit from city to city within a given culture.

This throws a lot of questions into your life which must be answered by you alone, does it not?

With that, dear reader, we come to the end of Part One.

To find out how the church ought to be raised up, we must learn how the church used to be raised up. *That* may surprise you.

PART II

How The Church Used To Be In:

Galilee
Jerusalem
Judea
Antioch
Galatia
Greece
Ephesus

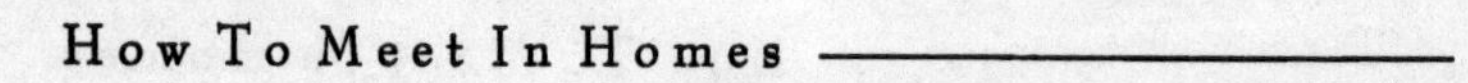

"There are more devout Christians who love the Lord Jesus Christ who **do not** *go to church, than those who do."*

5

Meeting, First-Century Style

How did believers in the first century meet? If there is a revolution, if there is a return to first principles, we *must* know. And when you see the way it was, be prepared for a shock.

Before you walk into one of their meetings, you must leave your organizational charts, your predisposition for organizing *everything*, your concept of the clergy, your practice of the pastorate, Sunday school, sermons, chairs, pews and church buildings . . . you must leave them all outside. This is *new* territory! Be you American, Chinese, Russian, Latin, Slavic, Nordic, Romanian or *Albanian* . . . this is *all* new territory; and ministers, ministries, mission boards and para-church organizations—*all are left outside. All!*

What happened in the first century was so radically different from what we do today, there really is no spectrum broad enough for comparison. Producing a hybrid—part now and part *then*—is not an option. It is either all or nothing. You may cross breed a horse and a donkey and produce a mule, but you cannot mix first-century ways with today's ritual and produce a beautiful girl named Ekklesia . . . a girl born to freedom, born to variety, born to function, and born to express Jesus Christ Himself.

Make room for a wholly new concept of the gatherings of the ekklesia and a new understanding of the ekklesia itself. You are about to see things long forgotten. You are also about to see the real power of the early ekklesia. Here is its true secret. *Here* is her mystique!

How did the ekklesia meet back in the heyday of Christianity?

THE CHURCH IN EMBRYO

Let us begin *not* at Pentecost. Let us begin with Jesus and the Twelve. How did they meet together? Can we call *their gatherings* a meeting of the ekklesia? Christ and twelve men, meeting, was the embryo of the ekklesia. In that embryonic fellowship in Galilee, twelve future church planters made the great discovery of *how to meet!* In those meetings those twelve men also *discovered* what the *ekklesia* was!

First, they met around Jesus Christ. For four years. On dusty roads. In living rooms. By the roadside. On mountain tops. They met. They fellowshipped. In many different places. But *always* it was the same: informal gatherings with *Jesus Christ* as the center.

Those meetings were the prototype of *all* first-century gatherings. They should be the prototype of all church gatherings! Those meetings were the foreshadowing of the ekklesia!

And what did those meetings look like?

The answer is simple. The disciples all carried with them a hymn book and prayer book. Come time to meet, they got dressed up, sat in neat little rows, all faces forward, with an aisle down the middle. Then Jesus put on His best clothes, making sure He always had a collar to put on that was turned around backwards. They all sang three songs, repeated The Apostles' Creed, sang another song, passed the offering plate, sang another song or heard a special from a quartet made up of Thomas, Mary Magdalene, John and Judas not Iscariat. Then Jesus stood up in front of them (they carried around a portable pulpit for Him) and brought a twenty-nine-and-a-half-minute sermon.

Do you really believe that? What?! You do not?! Then let me ask you the most imponderable question of all human history: Then *why* do you meet that way? And! Why choose to continue to suffer through the agonizing misery of the kind of meeting you attend?

How Jesus and the Twelve met together *was the first public, visible definition of the Christian faith.*

The world *sees* how we meet, and that is how the world defines, characterizes, interprets and understands who we Christians are. What did they see back then? They saw informality gathered around Jesus.

Here, try for yourself: Picture a meeting with Jesus Christ and the Twelve! Then try to fit that into anything going on today! Justify today's Sunday church service if you can, while holding in your mind's eye the Lord Jesus and the Twelve! It cannot be done. (It cannot be done by anything found in the New Testament either.)

If you are a minister (and especially if you are a minister who says "We really need to be New Testament"), then why in the name of sanity, honesty, and integrity do you hold meetings in church buildings on Sunday morning fraught with ritual that absolutely cannot be substantiated scripturally by even the most gargantuan leap of logic and fantasy? How dare you—how dare any of us—bring death to the ekklesia of the Lord Jesus Christ with a building and a ritual which erects an invisible wall between laity and those who minister. How dare you confine us to a ritual that does not allow us ever to speak or share or contribute? How dare you look at Jesus and the Twelve, yet turn around and leave us to be unfunctioning mutes? Place yourself in a room in Galilee. Give *us* that!

Consider for a moment what it must have been like to live with the Lord Jesus for three or four years. Do so and you are well on your way to understanding what meetings were like throughout all of the first one hundred years of church history. That is where we *must* return. In order to understand the spirit of ekklesia, the dynamic of our faith, and the magnificence of the meetings that prevailed in that day, start *there.*

Then Pentecost came. Twelve men who had lived with Jesus for three or four years suddenly became planters of the world's first ekklesia. Those three years in Galilee and Judea were their history and their experience. To them, ekklesia was three years sitting around with Jesus Christ! That Galilean embryo was about to be reproduced in Jerusalem . . . organically! Let us look at it, and let us see how the saints in Jerusalem met.

The Jerusalem Church

There was a period of about six or seven years when there was only one ekklesia in the world. Between about 30-37 A.D. the first and only church on earth was in Jerusalem.

The ekklesia had two places it met.

1. An Open Courtyard

Back behind the temple where almost no one went was a place where two of the walls of the city met, forming a corner. Someone had built a roof over a small part of that corner. People could sit under this shed to talk and visit. The first ekklesia the world ever knew confiscated that area and held daily meetings back there—around 500 to 2,000 went there at some point of time on the clock most every day.

Twelve men spoke back there under the shed. What did they speak about? They spoke about the Lord Jesus Christ! And when they finished doing that, they spoke about the Lord Jesus Christ! And when they finished doing that, they spoke about the Lord Jesus Christ!

Jesus Christ was *the* message of all the early *church planters.* (We will pursue this point later, as it is pivotal.)

Remove the centrality-of-Jesus-Christ message from ministry and meetings, and you can forget church life or organic meetings. *He* must be the center of everything . . . not in lip service, but in the dynamic experiential whole.

Try to imagine what would have been the reaction if one of those twelve men had been twitty enough to teach about the eyeballs, horns, claws, and bear tails in Ezekiel and Daniel. He probably would have been tarred and feathered. That mass of expectant people who gathered on the porch behind the temple wanted to hear about the Lord Jesus Christ.

Furthermore, they wanted to hear of a Lord who was the triumphant, resurrected, ascended, enthroned Lord, and *who lived inside of them* . . . and they wanted to know *how* to know Him . . . and they didn't want to hear about anything else. And Jesus Christ is what they got!

(After all, what would *you* talk about if you had lived with the Lord Jesus Christ for three years?)

Those people were electrified by what they heard. The twelve church planters were electric and electrifying.

Glory ran deep.

The listeners were Jews. In those days, the Jews were among the most extroverted, expressive, vivacious, effervescent, noisy, animated bunch of people on this planet. (Of course, in these meetings they never did any of that. They sat there blank-faced. When Peter would tell some glorious story, they did not dare say amen or praise God because it might have upset the Presbyterians present or offended the sensibilities of the Episcopalians passing by. Did I mention I have a bridge for sale?)

Listen, dear reader, those meetings were *Hebrew* noisy, which was several decibels above your music box! Even Italians would be hard-pressed to match them.

II. Jerusalem Homes

When those large, dynamic meetings ended, believers bathed in the glory of Jesus Christ poured out of there by the thousands and returned to homes scattered throughout the city.

They met again . . . in living rooms! In that simple gesture of meeting in someone's living room, *the Christian faith made unprecedented history.*

The Christian faith was the first and *only* religion ever to exist on this planet that had no special buildings, no clergy, no one dressed in a costume, no one with a special vocabulary. This fact was true only once in all human history. *Only* once. It lasted for three centuries *only*.

How they met defined the Christian faith: the only templeless, clergyless and ritualless religion in human history! What a glory to the Carpenter and to our faith!

Rugged, poor, tired people were the clergy, the living room their temple, worn-out clothes their costumes. And Jesus Christ was the vocabulary.

What effect did those home meetings have on those who were present in the gatherings?

Those home gatherings were the epitome of informality. How informal? Why, as informal as twelve men sitting around in a living room or on a roadside, talking with the incarnate God. *That* informal.

Mark this. Mark it well: The church of Jesus Christ was born in informality. It ought to have stayed that way. It must be informal if it is to be captivating and meaningful to us . . . and to un-believers who wander in! If our meetings are to communicate to the world what the ekklesia is and what the Christian faith is, then those meetings must return to informality. Our faith *was* born that way! Informal, and organic to our specific culture.

It is a law of physics, chemistry, astronomy, and gravity, as well as a law of the spirituals, that if you put the Christian faith in a building, cover it with ritual, employ a clergy, take away the informality, outlaw the spontaneity, and end the functioning, *you cease having the ekklesia.*

It does not matter how perfect your theology, you have pretty well killed the *practice* of the Christian faith! You have also, by the way you meet together, proclaimed to the world in big, flashing, red and yellow lights that you have got one very *dull* religion.

You may boast of your great past history, your traditions. You can tell us of all the great contributions your movement has made to church history. You can boast of your seminaries and the thoroughness of your theological training. You can tell us how skillfully your organization functions. Do so until the trumpet sounds; but, for the simple believer, you have killed the glorious daily reality of the ekklesia and, in that process, killed the dynamic of our faith. An experiential understanding of what our faith is comes close to disappearing. You lose the most significant, practical elements involved in the meaningfulness of Jesus Christ indwelling the believer. Functioning under the headship of Christ in the body—by the body—is lost.

But most of all, you deprive the body of Christ from ever discovering the intense love that saints can have for one another. You destroy all foundations for the experience of the community of believers.

That intense love is born, blossoms and grows *only* in community, and in an atmosphere where the centrality of Christ and the knowing of Him intimately is central. Lose those elements and you lose all bragging rights to any kind of weight to our faith. Lose those bragging rights and what do you really have to offer that is practical reality in the Christian faith? What you have left is mostly theory. And formality. And dust. *Dry* dust.

Dead ritual and polysyllabic theology really are not a lot to present to this planet. It surely does not give the world a very good definition of our wondrous and glorious Lord.

You can preach four times per week until kingdom come. You can tell us how wonderful it is to be the body of Christ, but until we *are* the functioning body of Christ, in a gathering, actually experiencing the life of the body . . . until then, you are blowing bubbles. Until then you will never end up with *anything* but an organization and a platform for weekly lectures. The ekklesia will never be seen, understood nor *loved* until she is experienced. Surely the Sunday church service (and all the add-ons the human mind can conceive in an effort to make Sunday church services endurable) will *never* produce *body life!*

If we could all go back to *one* evening in those Jerusalem living rooms and see what those brothers and sisters did and said, it would revolutionize the present-day practice of our faith and lead to a return to the excitement of being a Christian. A love for one another that is nothing less than supernatural would eventually blossom among Christians *again.* We would stand in wonder and awe of our Lord Jesus Christ. We would rediscover what has been virtually unknown in the faith for the last 1700 years. We would have finally figured out what made our faith so dynamic back then.

> When Christ as the center of our meetings is taken away, when you take away our living room meetings, when you give us a clergy, when you perfunctorily deliver lectures which do not show us the depths of the riches we have in Christ, when you do not show us how to experience Him both individually and corporately, in the depths, when you leave us nothing to do but sit and stare at a lectern in a civic auditorium that has funny-looking stained glass stuck in the windows, or even if you get real bold and let us go back to the living room meeting *but* only with the prerequisite that we have a leader directing us in what amounts to a miniature of the Sunday service . . . when you do all that to us, you have taken away our birthright and given a distasteful expression of what "Christian" means, to us and to the world!

I have a suggestion: Let us abandon this whole mess.

What made those temple porch meetings and those living room meetings so fantastic and glorious? Fearless men thundering a message to the redeemed of revelation of a risen, ascended, enthroned, reigning, exalted and glorified Lord! The people, hearing, were out of their minds with joy, and went home to living rooms, packed out and overflowing with people sharing what Jesus Christ meant to them! They sat there on the floor of that living room, sometimes until the wee hours of the night, singing, praising, worshiping and *sharing* about their Lord. What Lord? A Lord who lived *inside* them!

That was *ekklesia* to them!

Jesus Christ was the center of that people. He was the energy and rocket fuel of their lives. He was the topic of those gatherings. Most of all, this indwelling Lord became the leader of those meetings.

The Churches in Judea

Of course, this all changed when the ekklesia in Jerusalem shut down and everyone fled out into the towns and cities of Judea because of persecution, right?

One day a gentleman from Tarsus, Saul by name, came to Jerusalem and reigned terror on the world's only ekklesia. The twelve church planters went into hiding, while Saul caused not only the exodus of the Jerusalem church, but inadvertently also caused the planting of scores of churches in Galilee and Judea.

You know what happened out there in those smaller towns. The fleeing Christians settled into these towns and built buildings with steeples on top; they called pastors, salaried them, showed up on Sunday morning at 11 a.m., lined up benches in neat rows, and sat in silence for the next one hundred years while someone overloaded them with sermons.

They did not? Really? Then let me once more ask the most earth-shaking question ever posed: If they did not, then why do we?

The apostles were in hiding. Believers were scattered all over Palestine. What actually happened?

In living rooms all across Judea and the environs, the life of the ekklesia sprang up.

The meetings? Just like the home meetings in Jerusalem. That includes informality, no ritual, no clergy, and no pastors.*

Later the twelve church planters slipped out of Jerusalem and began traveling around Judea, paying short visits to all those new ekklesias. And just where did these twelve men get the idea of an itinerant ministry? From their Lord, who itinerated across Galilee for over two years.**

Do not think the practice of an itinerant ministry ends in Judea. The story of itinerant ministry sweeps across the first three centuries of church history. The traveling church planter—the extra-local worker—was a quintessential hallmark of the first-century ekklesia. He disappeared some time in the second or third

---

* *They would have to wait 1500 years before the pastor concept came into being. True, the word pastor appears in the New Testament, but because a word appears in Christian writing 2,000 years ago does not mean that when we use the word today it has the same meaning. Can you find anyone in the New Testament who was always the speaker, who delivered funeral orations over the dead, who presided over marriage rituals, who was the sole person baptizing the new converts, who went to a seminary, who presided over a liturgical service, who was salaried, who patted old ladies on the hand, who was the sole person responsible for visiting the sick, who was almost always dressed up in a suit, who prayed in a funny voice, who was hired and fired at the whims of a congregation, and who stood at the very center stage of all that there is of the Christian faith? If you can find that man in the New Testament, I'll eat my Stetson hat! Such a person never existed until the Reformation, which was 500 years ago. At that time he was invented by men without any thought of trying to justify his existence scripturally. He is a man-made tradition that grew up out of the expediency of reformers who were working shorthanded.*

** *Trans-local, non-local, extra-local, traveling: itinerant.*

century and, until he reappears, the Christian faith is never going to work the way it is supposed to.

Note the two central characters on the first-century stage: (1) God's people and (2) traveling church planters.

Keep that simple concept in mind as we move on in this unfolding drama. God's people, homes, planters of the ekklesia—a simple concept, is it not? Well, it shook the world. When we gave it up, the world shook no more.

Now, let us leave the incredible doings in Judea . . . the story of scores of "layman-led" churches and "people-functioning" ekklesias. But keep your eyes open; why, we may see a church building and the John Calvin Sunday ritual, pastors and pews, and silent people sitting in neat little rows, listening—forever listening—to Sunday morning sermons . . . any time now.

Keep a sharp lookout for such goings on as we go next to see how Gentile Christians met in Antioch.

"I must believe in the Apostolic Succession, there being no other way to comprehend the irrelevance of clergy and ritual except that these were passed down to us by the Apostle Iscariot."

—anonymous

6

Antioch

Antioch, the farthest city to which church life came after the Jerusalem church dissolved. This city, located on the Mediterranean Sea, was one of the largest cities of antiquity. The ekklesia began there under most unusual conditions. Young, zealous believers, recently fleeing from Jerusalem, hit town and, not finding enough Jews to proclaim the gospel to, preached that gospel (perish the thought) to us uncircumcised heathen Gentiles. (For which we are forever grateful!)

Here is one of those few instances where *secular* history tells us a little about *church* history. There are secular records left to us, from the second century, telling that Christians in Antioch lived in one particular section of Antioch, a section of the city known for its poverty. Estimates of the size of the Antioch church during the second century go as high as 10,000 believers.

How did this church gather? Well, there is a very telling sentence in Acts that speaks volumes about how believers in Antioch met. The story goes like this: Barnabas and Paul had just returned from their trip to Galatia. Here the book of Acts makes an off-the-cuff remark, ". . . and the whole ekklesia came together *in one place*." This can only mean one thing.

The ekklesia in Antioch did not often "all come together *in one place.*" Generally, the church met in homes all over the city. Only on special occasions did all in the ekklesia in Antioch come together in one place.*

We do not know how many actual *leaders* the church in Antioch had when Paul and Barnabas returned from Galatia, but we do know that two years earlier there had been five! (Barnabas, Paul, Lucius, Manaen and Niger). Who led all those home meetings? Those home meetings, scattered around the city, were not being *led.* Those very uproarious Gentiles . . . free of all law . . . were not sitting in neat little rows with a speaker up front. *They* were enjoying themselves. *They* functioned in those meetings. They *were* the meetings.

We, in turn, seem to be playing some kind of game on Sunday morning that could easily be entitled, "Substituting for statues!"

What were those home gatherings like?

These mere five men moved about in the city, visiting the house meetings from time to time, ministering Jesus Christ. That was the closest thing to a "professional" ministry that existed—temporal, spontaneous, sporadic, unpredictable.

What are we seeing here? An ekklesia, quite large, with members meeting in homes all over the city. And how, pray tell, did they meet?

Well, Barnabas came into the living room wearing this long, bejeweled robe of white linen and twined gold. He had this pope-like hat on, and in his hand he held a hooked shepherd's staff. He went around the living room kneeling at certain "stations" where icons were hanging on the wall. The service itself was an elaborate, highly ritualistic, *two-hour* dramatization spoken in an unintelligible language. The

---

**See* Rethinking Elders, *by Gene Edwards, SeedSowers Publishing House.*

people stood for the entire two hours saying nothing, just staring.

You do not believe that?

Well, you should, because the Eastern Orthodox church—the Anatolian branch—claims that is exactly how first-century Christians in Antioch met! They even claim their meetings have not changed in *1900* years.

Silly, you say? Maybe even insane to make such a claim? Well, we Protestants swear up and down that first-century believers met *exactly* the way Protestants do today! (Of course, we—like the Catholics and Orthodox—have no problem at all ignoring history.) That John Calvin invented our miserable ritual just 400 years ago is never mentioned. We Protestants meet in a New Testament way, the facts be . . . er . . . the facts be darned! Come on folks, let us all stop blaming Peter or Barnabas or Paul for this villainous deed called the Sunday church service!!

Leaving Antioch, we join two church planters on their first trip to go out and plant new churches. We will follow them to Galatia where we get an eye-opening look at how God's people meet out there in the heathen world. Gentile meetings in the Gentile world, first-century style.

What follows is the most important chapter in this book, and one of the most important chapters I will ever pen.

"If you speak the truth when everyone else believes and is practicing the opposite, make sure you are sitting on a very swift horse."
—Turkish proverb

7

Four Gentile Churches in Galatia

Paul and Barnabas left Antioch during the month of March, crossing by boat to the island of Cyprus, and from Cyprus they moved on to an area called Galatia, finally stopping in a town called Antioch of Pisidia. If the dates set by most scholars are correct, they came to that town, raised up an ekklesia, and then left town, all in four months!

Four months?

These two men are not evangelists. They are not there, primarily, "out to win souls." Not by the wildest stretch of the imagination are they the modern-day concept of pastor or missionary. These men have two characteristics. They are "movers-on" . . . that is, they are *itinerant.* (Such men were nicknamed "wanderers" in the second century.) And secondly they raised up churches.

Itinerant church planters!

These two *mover-on-ers* are also not centered on appointing elders. Nor are they particularly organizational minded, wanting to raise up a church, choose elders, get organized, and . . . *maybe build a building?* They were *not* in town primarily to get people saved. They came into that city for one purpose: to raise up the body of Christ, the ekklesia. They were there to bring forth a beautiful girl! They were *church* planters.

The *beginning*—the birth—of the ekklesia in Antioch of Pisidia was everything. How those Gentile believers met together that *first year* charted the course of that church for centuries. (The beginning is everything.) She and all the Gentile churches of that era held their course pretty well for over 200 years. It took a Roman Emperor to get her off course.

What were the meetings in that ekklesia in Pisidia like?

Remember, everything that happened in Pisidia happened in four months! That is, from the beginning until the two men departed was a total of about 120 days!!

"Catholics, did Paul come into a meeting wearing priestly robes?"

"Episcopalians, did the early church meetings have robed priests coming down an aisle in a processional with flags and chants?"

"Churches of Europe, when Paul came into the living room, did everyone stand up?"

"Presbyterians, did Paul stand behind a pulpit in someone's living room, with his shirt on backwards?"

"Baptists, was Paul all dressed up in his 'Sunday best' when he walked into that living room?"

And the believers? Pews? Faces forward? Calvin's church service? A few chosen songs? Mute laymen? A sermon?

It is only as we grasp the true picture of the first century that we begin to understand exactly what the ekklesia really was; and, for sure, it had *none* of the above trappings. *None!*

Look at these new believers. They were so poor,

it is beyond our comprehension. People lived each day to lay hold of enough grain to get through that day. Maybe they had one change of garments per year. They were ninety-eight to ninety-nine per cent illiterate. Their income in a year was equal to what you make in a day. But that does not mean they had money. They didn't. Most never used money. Those people bartered virtually everything!

The wealth, the money, was in the hands of one per cent of the population: the wealthy plus the middle class (the merchants). These two classes of people made up no more than one per cent of the population. *They* had money. The rest? Half were slaves and the other half were the "great unwashed." One percent had money. About ninety-eight to ninety-nine percent did not! And Galatia was a particularly poor area! The people owned nothing. They had nothing.

Holding that in mind, remember that we today see these people as the legendary *first-century* Christians.

See them stuffed into a room that has, maybe, one window. All sat on the floor. The sweat of the day caused their clothes to stick to their bodies—Paul and Barnabas included—for those two men, like everyone else present, came to the meeting after a hard day's work. Tired, if not exhausted; dirty, if not smelly, they, too, sat down on the floor. (That's what people did then. They sat on the floor! If you go visit some areas of the world today, you will discover the people living there *still* sit on the floor, in their homes!)

Did Barnabas and Paul function to the exclusion of all others? Did only Paul or Barnabas announce the songs, while everybody else sat quietly? If so, when those two men leave town, this ekklesia is going to collapse!

But Paul and Barnabas did not take that approach. From the beginning they raised the church up to survive . . . *without.* Without what? Without books, pastors, educators, literacy, Bibles, Bible school, buildings . . . without *anything!* But mostly *without* clergy *or* leaders. Everything those two men did was done in the light of the fact that they would be there only a few weeks! Yes! All things pointed to their *departure*—abandoning a body of believers *without any* leaders and with no designated leadership. And soon!

In an earlier chapter you were asked, "Can a revolution in how we meet be brought to a traditional church of our day?" The answer is yes. Absolutely. But only when properly *motivated.*

How can a church be motivated? Easily!

Everyone will know that in six months the church will be left alone without *any* leaders. Furthermore, the church will give up all use of the auditorium for two years! *That is* motivation.

The only problem left is finding (1) a pastor willing to lose his job and (2) a people willing to be left without leadership, who will abandon the church auditorium and meet only in homes *without* leaders of any kind!

That is all the motivation required!

Did Paul just preach—everyone else not talking, the meeting ending with a prayer, the mutes all filing out and going home?

Well, heathen did not act that way. Heathen, ex-heathen, neo-heathen and semi-heathen came into that home chattering, laughing, and talking. They were noisy. Whatever singing there was, was homegrown, home taught, and easily interrupted. Interrupted by spontaneous laughter and talk. Whatever sharing there was, was also interspersed by the most natural and informal questions, observations, comments, laughter and banter. My money says Paul and Barnabas made sure that their messages *were* interrupted with questions and comments. They designed the way they talked to bring this about! Furthermore, dear reader, sharing, singing, praying, talking and chattering went on *after* the message ended.

No set time to go home. Fellowship before, during and after ministry.

If you question this, then go to any place on earth where Calvin's Sunday ritual is *not* known . . . tell the people nothing about ritual, get up to speak . . . you will find yourself not in a monologue but a dialogue—no, a poly-logue as everyone joins in on the message, with comments, chatter, banter and laughter!

Among those heathen converts there were no concepts of Jewish ritual and certainly no Protestant or Catholic "worship service."

(And when Paul and Barnabas departed? Those Gentiles experienced *functioning*, on their own, after that!)

Never forget this: These people have fallen in love with one another. See them! Holding on to one another for dear life. They are 500 miles from the nearest other church! They are with one another all they can be, everyday. *This* close relationship, this love, powerfully affects the way the meetings are expressed.

Paul speaks, and he gets interrupted. When he finishes, there are questions and discussions. Actually, a buzz is more likely. Later Barnabas and Paul sit around and tell stories. Everyone laughs and *everyone* participates. The meetings cannot be more informal. Songs are started by everyone . . . and anyone. Sharing is spontaneous, informal, real, interrupted, interspersed and unexpected.

But even these glories are eclipsed by the mind-boggling fact that after only four months, Barnabas and Paul are going to leave those people . . . without cohesive ministry. *Four months!*

Think of it! All those illiterate people left with nothing but the *memory* of the gospel Paul and Barnabas preached to them during *that short time.* Their fierce love for one another is all they have, plus the sight and centrality of Christ before their eyes, and *living in their spirits!*

This was the Christian faith, first-century style . . . Gentile version!

Never think that when Barnabas and Paul walked out that door, then *elders* suddenly appeared. Or that the ekklesia just sat there, quietly, mouth shut forever, while elders preached them to death for the next century.

Elders did not appear.

When those two men left town, the ekklesia was a headless wonder! To say it was a non-clergied, lay-led church is an understatement. She only barely passed muster as a cohesive unit. But she had elements going for her we know nothing about. That day when the two church planters departed and membership dropped by two, the people kept on meeting. *And* loving one another. And caring for one another. *Only* four months of help, and the ekklesia never skipped a beat!

Just when do you think elders appeared? *Not once in Scripture are elders appointed at so early a stage in a church's life.*

There were no elders, there were no leaders. Those folks were on their own.

That next year—being left all alone—*is absolutely essential* for *any* ekklesia. Without that dramatic time, they would never have discovered for themselves *how to meet.*

But they *did.* They discussed how to meet—no one taught them!

On their own, these laymen and laywomen learned how to survive, bring ministry, sing, share, testify, meet needs, care for one another, and meet under the headship of Jesus Christ.

God give us this kind of beginning for churches . . . again.

Do you dare contemplate a church with a beginning like that? Do you dare dream of a people who would try such a venture? Could we believe they might even be *eager* and *excited?* Taking a daring plunge into such irreversible unknowns . . . and being excited about it!!

Well, that is exactly the price that must be paid by (1) people and (2) a church planter, if you are ever to discover *how to meet!* That discovery—how to meet—belongs to God's people alone, with *no* outside interference.

The number of adults present in that church was probably no more than around fifty. If you want to be really charismatic-minded and imagine big, push it up to one hundred, no more.

Do you endow these ex-heathen with our mindset? Please do not. These people are not going door to door witnessing. They are not Bible scholars. They are not "into" the Christian *family* as a central theme of the church. They are not "into" sending their kids to college. (Excuse me, a Christian college!) There are no Christian counselors on staff. No minister of music . . . not even a song leader. No pastor! No Bibles. No missions committee. No women's mission society. No political involvement committee. No building. No budget. No money. No education. Few can read. No Christian literature. No songbook. No books. Heathen! Ignorant heathen! Saved. For four months drowned in a cataract of the revelation of Jesus Christ . . . now on their own, to sink or swim . . . with no safety net, no escape hatch, no "911" to call in case of catastrophe. They have been abandoned with no contingency plans for rescue in case of utter failure!

What is the hope of these ex-heathens? What is their secret? This: By the time Paul and Barnabas departed, (1) they were awash in the knowledge and experience of Jesus Christ, and (2) they functioned.

They *functioned.*

In the meetings believers *were* the meetings. Outside the meetings, they cared for each other because they were in love with one another. And they fellowshipped with their Lord.

In the first century, the individual experience of a Christian with his Lord (and the corporate experience of believers with their Lord) was reported in the meeting.

The meeting was constituted of Christians reporting their daily walk and experience with Christ. In our age, we come to a meeting to get our empty bucket refueled. In their day, they came to a meeting to report out of the overflow of their lives.

There is a world of difference.

This experience of love for one another and their Lord was all they had.

Well, they had one other thing: The circumstances they found themselves in when left on their own caused them to be *highly* motivated.

May their tribe increase.

Those wonderful people have one thing on their minds: *survival.* They are holding on to one another for dear life. They have now been thrown on one another, totally dependent on each other for that survival.

Dear reader, you ought to have the privilege of seeing the likes of that! How would you like to be *that* motivated?! Thrown into these circumstances changes believers more than a thousand years of "going to church" ever could. Then and now!

These saints cared for one another with an intensity today's church member *has never seen.*

They did not have any choice, did they?

If one is sick, they are all sick. If one is falling away, they all feel the pain. They are a body of believers, moving, breathing, functioning, changing, adapting. Fluid! Flexible! *Forced* to be *creative* . . . each *forced* to lead out in some specific areas when a need or crisis arises.

When they meet, *all* of them carry the meeting. All the body, caring for all its parts. They are in love with *Him* and with His beautiful fiancee. In a word: They are the embodied, visible, living, breathing body of Christ.

And you prefer to "go to church" on Sunday?

Now the central question.

Dear reader, walk into a Baptist church next Sunday morning and ask yourself a simple question. Are these people madly in love with one another? Are they caring for each other? Holding onto each other? Listen, dear one, I am a Baptist minister. In a Baptist church in a typical city today people do not even know one another's names!

"Community" does not exist and is unheard of in virtually all present-day churches. In fact, our mindset does not even carry such a concept in its computer banks. A definition of that term does not exist among most believers, churches, movements and denominations.

By the way, a smile, a friendly handshake, and a warm and friendly atmosphere in a one-hour church service does not constitute "community."

We really are a long way from home, are we not?

The Lord gave one way by which His followers would be known: by their love for one another. When you walk into that first-century ekklesia, what you see are people who know one another, who are daily spending their lives together, helping each other in every way they possibly can. They are in one another's lives. When they say "brothers and sisters . . ." they are not kidding. That is no term—that is a living reality. These people, with all their problems in interpersonal relationships, are at the same time loving one another. And that love is very easy to see because of its very *intensity.*

If you do not have that element, in abundance, visibly overwhelming you, you simply do not have the ekklesia, no matter what you may think you have.

To state the obvious: Present-day Christians do not have that intense love for one another as a body of believers. We never will until we abandon the Reformation! The Reformation practices of the ekklesia were handed down to our forefathers and now to us. Let us bite the hand that fed us these Reformation practices! The present-day practice, understanding and conceptualization of "church" precludes an intense, overwhelming *love for one another!* (Little pockets of such love spring up occasionally, but they die away—killed by "church." These little groups come and go so quickly that they don't qualify to become statistics.)

We never will see this singular hallmark of our faith again until we revert to the principles of our founders, *Christ* and *the early church planters* . . . that is, a church raised up by (1) traveling church planters who center everything on Jesus Christ . . . and (2) a people left on their own.

Until we see this way flourishing again, there will

be no community, no "you shall know them because they love one another." Certainly, unless we revert to this divine pattern, we will *never* know *how to meet.*

Remember this: That love did not come about by Paul's saying, "Now, you have got to love one another." The source of that love does not belong to the visible creation. That love, and that camaraderie, that community, simply cannot come about by what is presently known as Sunday church. Or anything else that a building downtown at Broadway and Main provides. If you ever hope to see that intense love in the ekklesia, be sure that all there is of the Sunday morning rituals will have to be abandoned. *No ifs, no ands,* and *no buts.* No reservations, no qualifications. And no rescue contingencies in case of failure.

When Paul and Barnabas walked out of Antioch of Pisidia, the church did not see those two men again for *two years.* Contemplate that! But that ekklesia—against all odds—was still going when their two church planters came back!*

They survived two years alone because of glorious Bible studies, right? Well, because of seminaries, maybe? How about: the church survived because of a good choir and great, special music? No? Then maybe it was that warm, congenial, loving pastor?

Let us go visit a meeting a month after those two heartless church planters walked off and abandoned the dear ignorant souls who, if they would not have been given enough help in four months to even qualify for being on "the milk of the Word."

The meeting place, a house. Crowded, unventilated, the room stinks. Outside, the garbage on the street is rotting. It is piled a foot high. (They had to walk through this filth just to get into the home.)

---

* *Are you up to such things? If so, you will discover many things in such an experience. One will be: How to meet!*

Those people's hours of work started at four or five in the morning and ended at sundown. Only darkness ended a day's work, *if* work could be found.

(Two thousand years ago "full-time employment" was a concept not yet born. The wealthy hired someone when they needed them. That was the *only* employment for "the great unwashed.")

The room was composed almost exclusively of (1) the great unwashed and (2) slaves. The slaves were, of course, slaves. Some of the slaves and some of the great unwashed were farmers; and the farmers worked only four or five months out of the year. (They almost never owned the land. The wealthy owned virtually all the land, and the state owned the rest.)

The farmer was paid in produce from the land, not money. He then went to the market and bartered his produce for other products he needed. The rest of the year, because of the weather, he had no steady work. Any work he might get would come from standing in the marketplace hoping to be hired. When hired, he would work at that job for only a day or two at most.

There was virtually no one in that body of believers who had full-time employment. Perhaps a Greek or Jewish merchant. Merchants sold their wares to the wealthy, or bartered them to the poor. If there was a wealthy believer present in the meeting (and there very well may have been), he would be virtually the only one present with the true ability to purchase things with actual money.

Most of the believers present are living at the lowest end of human subsistence. Their life span is about thirty to thirty-five years of age. Because all of them are suffering from malnutrition, their physical height is between 5' and 5'4".

A month ago *these* people lost their founders and

their leaders. They have one another, an indwelling Lord, and an ability to function, to share, to love one another, and to care for one another. And they *love* to get together! That is all they have!

They are to be envied. Dare we emulate their courage?

My point: Those illiterates in Galatia did not have anything. They received a foundation in their faith from the apostle/church planter . . . centering on Jesus Christ. They stayed within the riverbed of Holy Scripture. Understand this: Their supreme goal and daily experience was knowing Christ, expressed and loved . . . horizontally and vertically . . . in the daily life of the ekklesia. Read the story for yourself!

This book is really not about methods! Despite its title, it is not a how-to book. The purpose of this book is to aid you in having a revelation of the need of the centrality of Christ and a vision of the ekklesia. And after that—hopefully—a radical, total revolution in your life!

The "how" is discovered in the crucible of church life. *How to meet* is found, void of man's invention. It comes from the bottom up. Burned in the crucibles of desperation.

We now bid the ekklesia in Antioch of Pisidia good-bye. Let us join Paul and Barnabas on their way to a town called Iconium.

"The Institutional church has killed only two kinds of people: Those who do not believe in the teachings of Jesus Christ, and those who do."

—Will Durant

8

The Foolishness of Church Planters

The story is the same in Iconium. In four months a church is started, the two church planters leave, and the people are abandoned to Christ. In Lystra the same story. Finally, in the small town of Derby, the two church planters again spend four months and leave.

Then the two men double back and visit the first three churches. By now the *Holy Spirit* has selected elders. (Paul and Barnabas only figure out who it is the Holy Spirit has organically raised up to be elders.)

What happens next? Oh, you know. Read it in any book about the early church. The two men become co-pastors and minister every Sunday for the next forty years. No? Oh, then each church calls some other man as pastor, and the pastor preaches to them for the next forty years? (That wondrous event will not happen for the next 1500 years!)

The two apostles launch a building campaign? No?

No! Those two cruel-hearted, callous men visit each church for a week or two. They then say goodbye and go back to Syria. Furthermore, these two cold-blooded, uncaring souls will not come back again for *two more* years.

These deranged "missionaries" have the audacity to walk out on all four churches. Tally it up: Each church got a total of four months of help in *four years!*

Are those two church planters mad? Cruel? Mad and cruel?

No!

Magnificent fools!

May their tribe increase.

What those two men did when they walked out on those four churches flies in the face of all missions, all mission boards, all para-church organizations, denominations, evangelistic movements, pastors and churches. Their mindset and ours are light years apart. No one in the traditional context of the church has dared to duplicate this! Not in fifteen hundred years! It is time to dare! Again!

What Paul and Barnabas revealed to us was . . . and is . . . and ever will be . . . the best way to raise up the church. This is the only way a people will *ever* discover for themselves *how to meet!*

Think not that the insanity of these two church planters is over. It gets worse!

"Throughout all the long history of Christianity there have been very few gatherings of the church when there were no leaders present, everyone announced their own songs, brought their own word, offered their own prayer, and then closed the meeting . . . all done without ritual, without direction, without someone looking over their shoulder, and in full freedom. Yet, that was exactly how the church met in ancient days."

9

The Churches Went Two Years without Help

Paul and Barnabas returned home to Antioch.

In a period of a little over four years, four churches had received less than one-half a year of outside help. At best, six months. That ministry was probably limited to no more than one, two or three meetings a week. That is a maximum of sixty meetings! (It was probably more like forty!) About forty to sixty meetings of help to last for four years. It happened. It can happen. It needs to happen again. It does happen.

This surely does fly in the face of "going to church" and listening to sermons for forty years . . . and *then sitting* for more of the same. You die, and your kids listen for forty years, ad infinitum.

We have to ask this question: "What on earth did these two men say that packed such a wallop? Just forty meetings? What was their message?"

THE MESSAGE

What kind of gospel did those men bring to four Gentile gatherings, buried up there in an obscure part of heathendom, hundreds of miles from any other believers? What possible message could produce such incomparable results?

Whatever it was, that message surely is not abroad in the land today.

There are dozens of schools of thought that rise up to give you an answer to this central question. A few are: power, eschatology, evangelism, spiritual warfare, Bible classes, etc. But those have been around for generations. Where are "Galatia-size" results of such ministry? It is *not* in *that* list. Such schools of thought cannot produce a Galatia, not on this planet at least.

Who among you really believe you have a message awesome enough that, if given only forty messages to deliver in four months—to savages—you could deliver those messages, sprinkle in a little practical help, and then walk out of there for four years? Walk out and leave nobody to help them? (And if there is someone out there who thinks he can, then why not do it??)

If you can, then in heaven's name do it!!

In fact, every minister should be subject to *this* test. Your gospel may be lacking if it cannot pass this test! If you think it can, give it a try.

A gospel of that portent does *not* exist in evangelical Christianity. If you think you have such a gospel, ask your church for an eight-month leave of absence, go to the heathen, and with no more than your Bible and your bare hands, try it.

Oh, and one other thing . . . as you walk out the door, give your gospel a *double* test. You are sure you have the gospel that can do this? All right . . . you have been ministering that gospel to your present church, have you not? Before you leave home to go to those poor heathen, test your gospel on *your* people! Now! Before you leave.

Have your people agree to have no ministry by clergy, no elders or deacons. Lock the doors on the church building. Your people are to get no outside help for *eight months*. Can you leave tomorrow? *Without* leaving your people *any* idea how to pull this off?

Why not try?

Think you can do that? If you do (and if you are a Westerner) and your church is flourishing when you get home, and that other church you are going to raise up in heathendom bare-handed is flourishing *four years* after you depart . . . I will write a book about how you did it.

Any takers?

Repeat: That kind of a gospel does not exist in the evangelical world.

Maybe the quality of those people was higher than the quality of Christians today? Brother, let us stop kidding ourselves. All over the world we Westerners spend generations on the mission field making sure we control such ignorant people. People that ignorant and that illiterate are not left on their own. The ministers and missionaries dare not do such things!

THE MESSAGE THAT WASN'T

The secret of the gospel did not lie in pouring out fact-filled teachings about the Bible. (Men did not have a Bible to teach from.) Time-honored as that practice is, it does not contain the ingredients necessary to raise up the church, Galatian-style! Virtually every evangelical, conservative, fundamental seminary on the face of the earth today says, "Get them into Bible study classes."

Try that in Galatia in 47 A.D. as your secret. Remember, you have four months!

What wonder, what power, what glory there was among those poor benighted people, and in their meetings. What stickability grew up among those barbarians emerging from just four months of ministry. Whatever that gospel was, it stands as an indictment against today's ever-perpetual ministry—sermon piled on sermon forever and forever. If modern-day evangelical Christians had taken the gospel to Galatia, we would *still* be there, preaching our sermons to stone-faced mutes . . . forever!

Repeat: you have got four months!

Today's mindset would strongly imply that if God's people did not "come to church" twice on Sunday, they would probably all fall into dire sin, join some unmentionable cult, and/or go off into worldliness.

Our present mindset implies that we believe that attendance at the one-hour Sunday morning ritual is the one ingredient that saves us Christians from becoming vile sinners within a week! And regardless of all, laymen cannot *ever* run the church. Our actions imply that the ekklesia must *never* be turned over to them. And certainly not four months after they are converted.

We do not trust laymen and do not believe in a lay Christianity. All of this is implied by our mindset and our practices.

Once more, why not test your gospel? Depart next week, Galatian style!

If we will not do this, then we are no longer implying; rather, we are stating as a fact: laymen cannot be trusted!

Is this not true, whether we admit it or not?

Something is amiss in our mindset!

What went on during those other three and a half years? Why not find out for yourself?

Nothing in history has changed so much but what this could be tried again!

Until we return to these basic, primitive ways, we will have a practice of "church" that is not attractive. Not attractive to believers or unbelievers. We declare a bride of Christ who is supposed to be beautiful. In fact, in our practice of her, she does not come up to being even snaggle-toothed, knock-kneed, freckle-faced and cross-eyed.

Try to find that girl today, the one whom Paul and Barnabas brought into being in Galatia. Start by looking at Sunday, 11 a.m. Examine the pews. See if she is hiding there somewhere. You may find her, perhaps in a village in Africa; but you will never find her in a John Calvin Sunday ritual, in a stained-glass building, among glazed-eyed spectators.

I would have you consider, long and hard, those four churches. Consider those short months of ministry. Place that scenario alongside what we have today. Comparisons are incongruous, if not impossible.

Will we rediscover a gospel which was that overwhelming? Yes, but not until we rediscover the centrality of Jesus Christ. Not until we replace a gospel that discusses things *about* Him with a gospel that *is Christ.* Not until we abandon a gospel centered on topics. Not until we embrace a gospel centered on *Him.*

There is a tremendous difference between a gospel centered on an "it" and a gospel centered on *Him.* Will we ever lead a people into a walk with Christ that is deep and enduring? Will we ourselves make that walk the passion of our own lives? Can we find a gospel that is so prevailing that it can do all that needs to be done *in just four months?*

Will we ever have men—workers—who can drop the peripheral topics of our gospel and dare to set a people utterly, totally free of *all* fear and rules? Will we see men called of God who will trust laymen to be the church, with no leaders present? Will we once more have a gospel that, delivered over so short a period, can produce an ekklesia that can get by for the next four years?!

Yes, we will. But if you wish to see it in your lifetime, then it requires that you abandon what you have now. Would you like to see a revolution? Then declare a gospel centered wholly on the Lord Jesus Christ—delivered in the electrifying knowledge that this gospel will be presented in an excruciatingly short time frame, with everyone knowing that at the end of the appointed brief time, the church will be abandoned, with no appointed leaders and no apparent leadership! That, dear reader, is a revolution, and it is a revolution charged with high drama, unbelievable motivation; and—most of all—it works, where nothing else does.

Paul and Barnabas went home to Antioch and stayed *two years.*

What was happening to those four poor, neglected churches in Galatia? Well, it was not all tea and cookies for them. That four-month gospel got tested to the uttermost. Hail, acid, flood and fire fell on those people, *and on that gospel.* Those four ignorant, lay-led churches fell under unbelievable attack!

What do you think? Do you think they made it? You do? Then why do you continue . . . ?

"Men occasionally stumble over the truth,
but most of them pick themselves up and hurry off
as if nothing happened."
—Winston Churchill

10

You Call This Help?

What happened to those four churches, meeting in houses, in Galatia? On top of all their other disadvantages, they were invaded by super-legalists, waving official papers of approval from the church in Jerusalem, who came into the meeting and proceeded to condemn Paul by name, then condemn the Galatians. And then they introduced a heretical faith in those home meetings!

> There is a *fire* that falls on *all* men's gospel. Most men have a gospel of wood, hay and stubble, and it is burned to cinders when the fire falls. I have a gospel that I preach to the Gentiles that is gold, stone and pearl. When the fire falls on the churches I raise up, nothing burns!

A man said that. He meant it. Can you say that? If so, then test it the same way Paul did. Four months! Then leave!

Paul, accompanied by Silas, went back to those four churches soon after that firestorm. What happened? What thin membrane of a destroyed church did they find? Paul and Silas must have had to spend *years* with each of the four churches straightening out the problems and "growing them up in Christ" all over again! What an insane mess those four ekklesias must have been in! I hear you say, "Years of ministry will be needed; and good, strong biblical doctrine needs to be preached here. It will take years to dig out of this catastrophe!"

If you are a minister and, perchance, you have a gospel as awesome as Paul's . . . see if it can pull off the following.

The four Galatian churches were basket cases? Not so! Paul and Silas hardly stayed long enough to say hello to those illiterate heathen.

Read it and weep!

The two men came in, did a little ministry, and, like a couple of lunatics, off they went into the wild blue unknown with no fear at all about the future of the four assemblies. Either they were crazy, or we have a very big hole in our understanding of how the church ought to be. And do you think their lunacy stopped here? Just wait. Now these two men go beyond lunacy.

The two men do something that is sheer madness.

The four churches had one and only one hope when their two church planters departed . . . *again!* A young man, a "minister" who had risen up in the church in Lystra, and had gone around helping all four churches. Boy, did those four churches need this young man. But, the two church planters stole him! They took the young man away with them!

Reread that: They stole the only help the four churches had. I suppose Paul was just not into "what the church needs today is *more* good solid preaching." By any known standards, these two church planters were certifiable maniacs! They deserved to be excommunicated! What unmitigated gall to rob the churches of the one human being who was showing signs of being able to minister to these desperately needy people.

Someone around here is way off track. You figure out whether it is us or them.

(The young man's name? Timothy.)

What does this audacious act show us?

In answer to our desire for ekklesia life, these two men show us the centrality of the church planter to the kingdom. Not evangelist, not pastor, not prophet. The central figure is the itinerant church planter.

The church planter of the first century did not see any great need for a lot of *local sermons!* Paul saw Timothy as a man *not* needed in Galatia. Repeat. Those four churches, recently savagely attacked . . . did not need Timothy! Or anyone else!! Paul was not thinking as we think. We think (1) pastor and (2) Bible student. Those two ideas would not be born until (1) fourteen hundred years later, and (2) eighteen hundred years later, respectively. Paul looked at this itinerant young man and saw "*church planter.*" "The churches do not need this man to minister locally. There is enough of that within the body itself." What this planet really *needs* are *church planters!* Paul actually thought the Galatians had no need of Timothy's services. He thought, instead, "Timothy needs to travel with church planters." That is how church planters were raised up, traveling with church planters!

Dear reader, don't think "pastor." Don't think "Bible school." Don't think long years of "getting preached at and taught at." Think "church planter." Itinerant, mobile, moving, visiting, departing *church planter.*

With a church planter *who has grown up in church life*—that is how a church begins, and he is the secret to *how to meet.*

Watch Paul and Silas steal Timothy. This shows us the importance of beginnings. It was more important, in the eyes of Paul, to train this young man to be a church planter than it was to leave him there to minister to those needy people.

Is it really possible those churches were so well off that this outrageous theft did not strike them as strange? If so, is this not a view absolutely opposite to all the values we place on ministry today? Imagine churches as impoverished as these, yet so well off they could be abandoned wholly to the Lord and His people after just a few days' visit.

May such churches live again on this earth.

Now look at our math one more time.

Four years with four months of ministry. After four years?

A week or two of help.

Paul then stole Timothy, their only gifted speaker, from their midst.

Call it five months of help in *six* years! We will now stop counting. Why? Because after that, the statistics get so unbearable, unbelievable and so embarrassing, we do not want to even think about it anymore!

I would like to point this out as the single most mind-boggling fact in church history.

You want miracles? You want power? Try pulling *this* one off in our day! *This* dwarfs all the miracles I have ever heard of.

Four months of meeting . . . and that was about it . . . for years and years and years.

How is this possible? Simple: Those four churches were functioning, with *all* meetings being in the hands of what we call laity. Put *that* in your organizational chart.

You who pick church planters by committee, put *this* down as a qualification for a church planter. Hold him to four months of ministry—per church—for a period of no less than six years!

It was possible then! But today? Sure, it is possible today. All you need do is give four months of ministry centered on Christ, depart with God's people knowing how to experience Christ and how to live by an indwelling Lord . . . then throw the ball to them. Oh, just make sure they discover *for themselves . . . by themselves . . . how to meet!* (Oh, by the way, all church planters in the first century experienced church life *before* ever having any part in church planting.)

Evangelism, First-Century Style

For those of you who are obsessed with the evangelizing of the world in our generation, please note that Paul raised up four churches in Galatia and considered the entire province of Galatia evangelized! It was the planting of an ekklesia, not numbers of people saved, that was the measuring stick of evangelizing.

(By "ekklesia" we mean the community of the believers, *not* a people meeting in something that looks suspiciously like a civic auditorium with weekly lectures delivered to a roomful of people, strangers to one another.)

Ours is strange thinking when compared to Paul's! Paul's thought is centered on establishing the ekklesia, *not* on soul winning. Note, too, this important fact: Paul evangelized in order to raise up churches. He did not raise up the church in order to evangelize.

The final end of evangelism is to raise up an ekklesia in a city! Evangelism has no great purpose beyond the establishing and growing of a local ekklesia in a specific city. Evangelism was never an end. Evangelism served the ekklesia. (May we one day get that very spirited horse back in his corral where he belongs.) Evangelism is a tool for church planting and church growth. It has no reason to exist in and of itself. Outside its use to plant a specific ekklesia in a specific town and to grow that specific church, evangelism should *not* exist!*

Paul considered a province evangelized and his main task over as far as evangelism was concerned. Evangelism rested with those meetings in homes.

The total membership of those four churches in Galatia probably was less than 200, total. What a value system. What a contradiction to our concept. Two hundred people gathering, in an entire province, and Paul considered that province "evangelized." Sure! The ekklesia—living, breathing and virile—was present!! One of these two concepts of evangelism—Paul's or ours—needs to be abandoned!

The planting of the ekklesia, by church planters, is waiting in the wings, waiting to be—in our day—center stage once more!

Paul, Silas and Timothy, staying only a few days in Galatia, desert the four churches once more. Where are they going? They have the gall to believe they can plant more neglected churches! In Greece. And they even believe such audacious neglect will not keep

---

* *Certainly if you are sitting in an airplane and the man sitting next to you is interested in knowing Jesus Christ, then, unquestionably, witnessing is proper, and winning him to Christ is the only correct thing to do. But the idea of welding together a force of people to witness, the sole end and purpose being only to save them from hell, with no thought of birthing a local "community of believers," has absolutely no precedent in Scripture and falls outside the mind of early believers. To be a Christian and to belong to the community of believers was one inseparable thought. Evangelism just to save would have been unthinkable by members of a local ekklesia.*

yet another four churches from surviving and flourishing!

The three men are quite mad, you know.

"There were very few Christians in the first century.
It is probable that this should have been true in all the centuries that followed.
The greatest problem Christianity faces today is that there are simply too many Christians."

11

How the Churches in Greece Met

Having learned from their brash experiment in Galatia—staying in a town for only four months and then abandoning those new churches in their infancy—Paul, Silas and Timothy head out to do the exact same thing over again in Greece. (*But, of course,* these men have learned their lesson! They will surely stay longer than four months the next time they raise up a church!)

They come to the city of Philippi. They stay three weeks.

Three weeks! Read it and weep!

That is not all. This man Paul (known to be a male chauvinist), leaves the church in the hands of a *woman!* (Of course, I am sure he would not let her speak in the meetings!)

The fact that Paul left the ekklesia in Philippi after only three weeks seems to prove beyond all doubt that lining people up in rows, climbing up to a pulpit in front of God's people and "preaching the Word to them" for the next five to six years seemed to be a *non-existent* concept in the first century!

Take your choice. A once-a-week, one-hour

meeting for a lecture? Or a sink-or-swim community of believers! The centrality of the early ekklesia was the message of Jesus Christ Himself. Coupled with that was the nurturing community of the believers that organically grew out of knowing Christ and meeting together.

What awesome thing is this?

The community of believers! It cannot be explained or defined, only beheld and experienced. It is God's people loving and caring for one another, and holding on to one another like crazy, plus hundreds of other elements, most of them inexplicable.

Paul, Silas and Timothy moved on to three more cities.

They came first to Berea and then on to Thessalonica. In both cases, they stayed about four or five months. (Obviously, they have still learned *nothing* about their past failure.) Five months, and they abandon the ekklesia.

They are being no kinder here than they were in Galatia. These men were stark raving mad and our methods are right . . . or they knew what they were doing, and we . . . ?

Here is the hallmark of first-century church planters. These men really trusted God's people. They trusted *laymen.* A quaint idea, is it not . . . trusting untutored laymen—only a few weeks old in Christ—to be totally and utterly in charge of a newborn ekklesia hundreds of miles from nowhere! Or was it an indwelling Lord those men trusted? Or better, was it an indwelling Lord who trusted those laymen? Either way, it is a trust utterly unknown in our age.

CORINTH

Now, we come to Corinth. Corinth was the great

exception. Paul stayed . . . ten years? Would you believe five? How about three?

Paul stayed in Corinth eighteen months.

Why so long? You call that long?

I used to live in a city in deep East Texas. The pastor of one of the city's largest churches had ministered in the pulpit of one church for over thirty years. (Corinth? No.)

Think of this: God's people in that city came in, sat down in total silence, and listened to that same man for over thirty years. They filed out an hour later, went home, and came back the next week . . . for over thirty years. Almost an entire adult lifetime! Were those people finally mature enough, adult enough, to take over functioning? On the day he retired, was that church any better off spiritually than the day he began? Had anything moved? Were the people *finally* prepared to do more than sit in neat little rows and *listen?* Were they now—at last—ready to at least function? Or was the whole orgy a goalless cycle that had no ultimate accomplishment—ending exactly where they had begun. Surely something should have emerged after thirty years. No, the same thing was to be done over by the next minister! Correct. The next minister spent virtually an entire adult lifetime preaching to those same people. He, too, retired. And nothing had moved. In over half a century. Nothing. God's people had simply come in, for a second lifetime, taking the place of their dead fathers, received some information, and filed out. The next minister preached there for thirty *more* years. When he retired, the church still had not moved or changed. They are now on number three.

Ours is a cycle without purpose or goal.

Dear reader, some way, this simply does not make sense! Is *this* not the *real* madness? One thing is certain: The pattern in Tyler, Texas—the town I call home—does not fit the way first-century Gentile churches were raised up. It *does* fit the pattern of the last 450 years, ever since Calvin lectured the people to death in the city of Geneva. Put those fifty or sixty years together. Compare that with eighteen months Paul spent in Corinth! Eighteen months is not long, is it?

Repeat, Paul was in Corinth eighteen months! Let us go to Corinth. They, more than anyone else, can tell us about first-century gatherings.

"The most boring thing ever thought up by the mind of man is the Sunday morning church service. It would be a lot more fun, and probably more edifying, to stay home and watch your washing machine go into spin dry."

12

The Greek Church that Overfunctioned . . . a Little!

The Corinthians met in the home of Gaius. Their number was not so great but what they could all fit in one living room. (It must have been a big living room.)

But the believers in the assembly in Corinth had this bad habit of two or three getting up and talking at the same time. Have you ever seen anything like that? If you have not, know this: You have a right to see such a meeting.

Huh?

That's right. Brothers and sisters can and do get *that* excited about the Lord Jesus Christ. The atmosphere is so infused, you have to hold onto your chair while someone else speaks. Such an interruption, in such an atmosphere, is no more out of place than it is at the breakfast table in your home.

I have been in many meetings where the first person speaking stopped to let a second person share something exciting about his Lord that dovetailed with the words of the first, only to see a third person entering in before the first person could continue on. I have seen two or three or four people do this, and it is so normal it is not even seen to be anything except . . . *normal.*

May you live long enough to be in such a meeting.

However, that was not exactly what Corinth was doing. All three were talking at once! Paul advised them to change to "one at a time," but he did *not* discourage interruptions. Read it for yourself!

This *never* happens in today's church! I wonder why? "Well, there was this fellow named John Cal . . ."

Corinth was overfunctioning, yes. But the present-day Christian can read the two letters to Corinth and never even understand what is being talked about. Everything about Corinthian meetings is so foreign to our experience, there are no grounds to identify with them.

Those who have experienced church life understand immediately the problems they were having in the meetings. Perhaps we have never actually seen these things happen, but we can identify with the nature of the meetings and are not surprised at these problems occurring.

I have been in many gatherings where we found it necessary to dismiss the meeting at midnight—not because anyone wanted to go home, but because some present had to be at work by six a.m. The meetings were full, even effulgent, rich, overflowing, and (interestingly enough) indescribable. I have also walked into many meetings with a message to share. At about ten p.m. I gave up the idea! Better things than a message were afoot.

Put these elements up against the Sunday morning "worship service." Somebody back there in the fourth century stole our birthright. You might just want to take it back again!

The Lord's people functioning in a meeting does more for the soul, for the spirit, for the church, for the kingdom than a hundred modern-day sermons.

On every occasion I have witnessed (and I have been in thousands of such meetings) where God's people were functioning, the church has always out-ministered the minister. If such a meeting begins to emerge in your church, dear minister, get out of the way and let it go; it will virtually always be richer than anything you could ever share. And even if it is a disaster, you have signaled to your people that you are willing to gamble on the laity the way Paul did! What you would have said may have been more profound, but it will not be more meaningful . . . not to His people.

One of the greatest church planters who ever lived (who spent eighteen months with an ekklesia in Greece) . . . a man who knew how to raise up a church . . . who spent more time with that church than any other . . . who was not a young apostle . . . and who had so many problems with this church . . . still *loved* that abysmal church!

With all their problems, he never took away their open meetings. Never once did Paul ever suggest ending open meetings. And never once in all he wrote to them did he mention *elders!* Certainly, then, elders did not step in and correct the situation.

The *letter* he wrote corrected the situation.

What if you received a letter from a church you had raised up and it advised you that brothers were getting drunk at the Lord's supper? I think the natural inclination would be to call a halt to this freedom in Christ and say "Stop!" thus placing the believers under human control and locking them into ritual's confines *and* ritual's *safety.* Every drop of blood in your being would probably rise up and say, "Put somebody over this situation! "

Nowhere does Paul say, "The deacons should take care of this," or "The elders should do so and so." The whole letter is addressed to the *whole* church.

Closing down those open meetings, in the first century, was a thought *never* thought! Even with people getting drunk at the Lord's Supper!

Paul did ask a *non*-local . . . itinerant . . . worker to visit Corinth. But Paul did not say to Titus, "Go down there and straighten them out!" Rather, he said, "Review with Corinth that which I have shared with them in the past."

In the midst of those Corinthian problems you see the humanity in brother Paul. After Paul wrote to Corinth, he became very anxious that the letter might have hurt someone! He wanted a report from Titus so much that he went to Troas to meet Titus ahead of schedule. But Titus did not show up. Paul was beside himself with concern for Titus' welfare and for that of the Corinthian church. Finally, Titus arrived. Paul later reported that he was relieved beyond words to hear Titus' report.

Titus gave Paul the one word he wanted so much to hear: "They still love you."

Paul rejoiced. The letter had edified, not destroyed! And church life went on. (That included rather boisterous functioning!)

This is the way church life is supposed to work.

Trip Two in Review

Paul and Silas forsook four churches. (*Paul* had forsaken eight in all.) The two men abandoned those churches and returned home to Antioch, Syria. Six years passed in all.

There were only eight Gentile churches in all the world. Eight!

Hear this, all of you who are evangelists and you who want to save the world in one generation (ignoring the fact that after you got the whole world saved over a period of one generation—forty years—

you really have not done a great deal because the number of newborns in the meantime would be larger than those you evangelized. Billions will *still* be unconverted by the time you are old!)

Sirs, look at evangelism through the eyes of Paul of Tarsus. It is not an evangelism of winning people to Christ; it is an evangelism of planting churches, one church in one city.

Paul is a lousy evangelist and needs to be rebuked . . . at least by our standards. He has raised up only eight churches on this whole planet! All the people in all those churches may not have tallied over three or four hundred. (The population of the Roman Empire was 75,000,000.) By all present-day standards, Paul was an evangelistic failure. True. But boy was he a planter of functioning bodies of believers.

Ask God which He considers of greater value . . . and which produces the greater *long-term* results!

Here is the man Paul whom we hold up as our reason (and our excuse) for all our evangelism. Please know that, in six years, birthing eight churches is all that man accomplished!

Also note this: He would make only one more trip. It would be—as the other two trips—to plant churches. *Three trips* in one lifetime. That is all. Just three. So on the third trip we can expect him to maybe plant at least a dozen churches? Six? Well, surely at least four more. No! He plants just *one! One* more church! That is all! Nine churches total. Put that in your evangelism mindset!

Take the totality of today's concepts of church practice, pick up those practices and concepts, then try to place them in the first century. Or try taking first-century practices and placing them in our age. Neither is possible! One of them must go in order to make room for the other.

Take your choice.

We have had almost 500 years of trying to practice our faith with a pulpit and neat benches all in a row. We have explored and exhausted the principle of "the big tongue, the big ear, and the iron derriere."

Give it up!

Revert to our faith *first-century style*.

In so doing, let us make functioning, caring, loving, and the centrality of Christ our end. Unless the totality of Calvin's way to meet is utterly abandoned, we will eventually be drawn back into the mess we are in, there to go on repeating that ritual *forever!*

Nothing short of revolution is necessary. Major revolution.

Today there are about 400,000 Protestant churches in the United States. Virtually every one of them has a preacher who is preaching God's people into spiritual death for one hour per week.

Let us draw a parallel to today's situation. Imagine a football coach talking to a team of listening athletes . . . forever. Where would football be?

We are not statues. We are living, breathing creatures whom Jesus Christ indwells. According to Paul of Tarsus, the church belongs to Jesus Christ and to all the saints. It does not belong to ministers. When we are set free, it is impossible for you to imagine how glorious and dynamic the church can be when meeting under the direct headship of Jesus Christ.

Here is a question for all of us: How many of the 400,000 churches in America will *ever* need this verse:

> "When one of you is sharing in the meeting and someone else gets really excited because they have had an insight into their Lord, let the second

> person interrupt with that which is flowing out of his spirit. After the second person has finished, let the person who was speaking first continue on with what he has to say."

I have money in my clothes that says, not *one* of them!

I hope that changes, but it will *never* change if you try to make it an add-on to church practice. Either Calvin's pulpit and ritual prevails, or functioning prevails. Otherwise, Sunday church will snuff out the expression of the body of Christ. In the long run, "Sunday church" snuffs out *all things!* It will take some bold, courageous men and some *avant-garde* lay saints to lead the way.

The ekklesia of the first century needed that verse. Does yours?

Will the church in Albania ever need this verse? Dear Lord, in heaven, I hope so. May the need of that verse arise in all lands where we have Americanized the church. And in all places where meetings of His people have been *John Calvinized!*

Can the typical church and the typical minister of today change? Can these fundamental pillars of Protestantism,

pulpit
benches-in-a-row
two songs
a prayer
two more songs
offering
one more song
then a sermon

. . . be dropped?

The question is yours to answer.

May I suggest this battle cry: Christians of America, Christians of the West, and especially Christians in the southern hemisphere and Christians in the East . . .

Unite!

Throw off your chains.

You have nothing to lose, except the place you take a nap every Sunday.

We have one last place to look as we observe how first-century believers met. Let us take a close look at the ekklesia in Ephesus.

*"Stepping out of institutional Christianity is not an act, it is a calling. Only those who feel called to do so should **ever** depart the traditional ways of the practices of the traditional church."*

13

Ephesus, More Surprises and More Madness!

Paul goes home to Antioch. What Paul does next is as insane as everything else he has done. As he prepares for his third journey, he pulls *the best men out* of each of the eight Gentile churches!

How cruel can one man be?

Today our seminaries present the men of the New Testament as being committed to the preaching of the Word of God. So we leave the seminary, line God's people up in rows, tell them to be quiet and not move, and then we preach to them until they are zombie-ized!

Paul had no such view.

This deranged man is again stealing the men best at leadership and ministry—yes, the men most adept at ministry of the Word!

Too bad about you folks out there in those eight churches. It seems you do not need to be preached to death after all. *And Paul, who is obviously not a present-day traditionalist, thinks he needs planters of churches worse than you need sermons.*

Paul picks eight men, the creme de la creme, out of the churches and tells them to meet him in Ephesus. Why? So he can train and raise up itinerant church planters. "Wanderers!" Paul's view does not include having a great deal of ministry within churches. He is concentrating on raising up itinerant workers who can make short visits to each of these churches and on raising up new churches. He knows the churches minister to themselves.

Taking those eight men left the churches with less ministry than they had before. Boy, they already had very little of what we today call ministry. Paul, you obviously have one very weird value system. Brother, what you need is a good seminary education!

If you ever encounter a free-wheeling experience of the community of believers, you will see that community is first in the life of the believer, with ministry flowing *out of* community. Sometimes you will see the flow change directions, and community will flow out of the results of ministry of the Word.

Unfortunately, the present mindset of evangelicals provides neither. In its place you find ministry, ministry, ministry—ad infinitum—with *no* community!

Ephesus And Eight Men

After staying almost two years in Ephesus, Paul and this company of young men he brought to Ephesus with him—whom he trained during those years—spent *two more years* traveling into the nearby towns of Asia Minor. Paul took these apprentices with him.

Those eight men made brief visits back to the churches from time to time. The churches are essentially on their own, eventually becoming self-sufficient in their own ministry, with intermittent help from Paul the "wanderer" and some of the other eight workers.

Ministry comes out of the body itself if a church is properly raised up. In the years ahead, these men will "wander" on out into new territory, planting churches in other cities and other countries.

Nor did they stay anywhere very long.

Lord God, give us back our "wanderers."

Eight men trained by Paul at Ephesus will duplicate Paul's ministry. Those eight men will be itinerant, moving into a city, staying a short time, raising up a church, and (instead of trying to evangelize that city right down to the last human being) will leave the city and leave the church.

Each new church, like the ones before it, will be totally in the hands of newly-converted, untutored laymen, most of whom are illiterate. These young *apostlettes* will return to those churches and encourage them, but such return visits will be unbelievably rare.

It almost seems like a minor event when these traveling church planters do return to the ekklesia to aid God's people in their progress in Jesus Christ. (Meanwhile, back in Greece and Galatia the eight Gentile churches are suffering from lack of eight good preachers!)

All eight men (and Paul) obviously need a good rebuking. The para-church movements of today, for instance, would tell these men they will never save the world by this slow, wasteful approach to evangelizing the world.

Nine men are moving at a snail's pace, souls are going to hell, and the Gentile churches are anguishing from lack of the greatest need in Christendom: great pulpiteers!

Two value systems clash here. Look how opposite they are. Constant preaching versus seasonal ministry. A clergy-dominated church that really does not trust turning the entire church over to laymen, versus a lay ekklesia. A pastor in charge of all things in the church versus a people in charge of all things in the ekklesia. Sit-and-listen versus function-and- express.

Preaching of the Word of God—first-century style—was sporadic, spasmodic, itinerant, and certainly not scheduled by a certain day nor by the hands on a clock. Whence, then, came ministry for these poor souls? Ministry came out of the mouths, the hearts, the spirits, the tears, the souls of God's people. They gathered and shared in song, word and prayer. And *daily* in their lives they aided, cared for, encouraged, exhorted and passionately loved one another in their Lord.

Look at the "seminary" these eight men went to. See their *ministerial* preparation.

> (1) They got saved and grew up in the free-swinging body life of the ekklesia.
>
> (2) They each showed promise as men who might truly be called of God.
>
> (3) Paul called them out of their local assemblies to go with him to Ephesus.
>
> (4) He had them sit down and watch him raise up a church, from scratch.
>
> Each of these eight men had already watched the birth of a church once before . . . back in their own home town. But remember, each man was from a different town, in a different area of the Roman Empire, so each had an experience of church life different from the others.
>
> (5) Consequently, each had the privilege of swapping stories about church life in a half-dozen different cities and cultures. Those eight men

had the unparalleled experience of cross-pollinating their church life experiences with others!

Then the eight men watched church life begin and blossom in Ephesus and in the newly-birthed churches in the towns near Ephesus. They were not seeing anything new, just different; and this time they watched and listened a lot more intently.

Each of them had experienced an incalculable "love of the brethren." All of them knew exactly what it felt like to get only a few months of help from their church planter and then face the trauma-glory of making it on their own.

All eight grew up in lay churches where *how to meet* was discovered, not imposed.

All eight men already had experienced the depth and riches of ministry which come only from out of the body of Christ itself.

ASIA MINOR

Two years after arriving in Ephesus, Paul began to go out into the countryside and raise up churches in the small towns of Asia Minor near to Ephesus. He took the eight young men with him. *This was deliberate.* First they watched him in Ephesus *from the beginning.* Then they watched him—and helped him—raise up churches in the towns and villages of Asia Minor *from the beginning.*

Yes, they had all known ekklesia life years ago in their own home towns; they had been present at the birth of the ekklesia *from the beginning!* But now each of them had seen at least *three beginnings.* And they heard from one another about some five or six other *beginnings* in other provinces and other cultures. Now they were helping Paul raise up churches!!

This was their seminary education.

Their professors? *One* man, one *old* man. Beat up, but experienced. A church planter was their seminary!!

That is the way men called of God were trained and raised up in the ancient days; this is the way they must be raised up again in our day.

Church life has no hope of flourishing again outside this scenario.

Having sat at Paul's feet and watched him so thoroughly, the eight young men were finally sent out *on their own.*

Paul—as did the church planters before him—understood the importance of those first beginning days when a church is being born. That time of beginning is important for God's people, for the ekklesia, and for young church planters.

Beginnings are everything in church life. So are church planters.

Now it was to be these *church planterettes* who were about to lead out in those *beginnings!*

Under Paul's eye, under his tutorship, eight Gentile men became *sent-out ones.* Suddenly the Gentile world finally had its very own apostles!

If you are one called of God, young man, may the Lord be so merciful to you and give *you this* apprenticeship. Nothing else is really much good. Nothing else really works. This was hands-on, on-the-job training . . . designed by Paul, yet a duplicate of how Jesus Christ had raised up *Jewish* apostles. The Lord gave us twelve Jewish apostles by virtually the same means Paul gave the Gentile world eight more!! *What a picture!*

But what is the center of this picture?

It is not a Bible school or seminary. It is not people being preached to death, while not being allowed to move or speak during the funeral procedures! What is going on in Paul's heart? What guides his activities? Is it not this?

Church planters are needed *first*. Before anything else. Church planters! However, young men who go out to plant churches need to have been in church life *first*! You start out as an *ordinary* brother . . . in church life. Why? Like those eight young men, a man needs to be known by believers in the ordinary settings of every day life before going as a young worker with an old church planter.

Survivors of the crucibles of church life are the best candidates for Christian workers! Such young men, laymen *all*, first need the commendation and recommendation of the ekklesia where they live.

Eventually, they also need to show evidence of their call.

Finally, men who wish to be church planters should live in church life with an old church planter present. It is his to select them; it is his to train them. This is a must. Even if it takes much needed and valuable men away from the local ekklesia. Such young men need to go out from home and watch churches being raised up by a *very experienced* church planter. In other cities, and in other cultures.

Sit at the feet of a beat up old church planter! Watch how he deals with problems, answers questions, deals with boiling hot criticism. Watch his methods, his ways. But most of all, watch (1) his message and (2) how he *leads* a people into a deep, meaningful walk with Christ!

Then these young men must be set free! Set free by the old toothless wonder who trained them. (Yet still being allowed to draw help from their mentor, as needed.)

This is not just the best way to raise up workers, it is the *only* way found in the first century.

* * *

We have seen the first-century way of meeting. Now let us talk about how to *discover* for ourselves *how to meet* . . . in our day.

But the question keeps returning: Are you ready to abandon *everything* you do today? Everything?

I hope so, because this is exciting.

If we give up "going to church," what takes its place? Nothing less than a church organic to its environment. What does that mean?

"Men never do anything outrageous or wrong so completely and cheerfully as when they do it from religious conviction."

—Blaise Pascal

14

Shattering the Mind-Set

Have you ever been in a Buddhist temple? Probably not, but in a movie you saw someone go into a Buddhist temple, squat down, cross his legs and click two sticks together. Somewhere you saw how a Buddhist relates to Buddhism in a Buddhist temple. From this picture alone—wholly separate from any religious information—you got your image of what a Buddhist is! You even got an idea of what Buddhist teachings were and what those teachings lead to.

You have seen Moslems in a mosque. This, more than anything else, shaped your opinion of what a Moslem is, and what being a good Moslem leads to.

You have been in an Eastern Orthodox church service. You smelled the stinky smoke, watched the stone-faced priest and stone-faced people. From this meeting, with no information whatsoever, you got a pretty good idea of what the Eastern Orthodox stood for and what they believed. All this just by watching their meetings. Not very appealing, was it? Yet, going to that service is the very height and pinnacle of the expression of devotion for people in the Orthodox church.

You have seen a Catholic service, its black-robed priest, the mass. From this you learned about

Catholicism. But do you realize that what you actually saw was how the *majority* of Christians on this earth meet! The *majority!* The single greatest way Christianity tells the world what Christianity is . . . is the Catholic mass.

The Moslems and Buddhists and Hindus have seen the Catholic meeting, and they truly think that Mass is pretty much what the Christian faith is! Not a very good image of our faith, is it? It does not even get in the neighborhood of what is portrayed in the New Testament, does it?

Is a Catholic meeting your idea of our faith? Well, every time Catholics meet they define the Christian faith to all the world, and the world believes that kind of a meeting *is the will* of the Christian's God! The world sees and learns about our Lord in these vaulted cathedrals, chants, smoke, wafers, rituals and golden robes.

Dear Christian, we evangelicals also define our faith every time we meet on Sunday morning. What does the world see? It sees a God who wants us to dress up in fine clothes and who wants us to all sit quietly, face forward, stand up on cue at the sound of a guttural-throated organ, sit again, then lipsynch a few songs, sit again, and stare blank-faced for an hour.

(Remember, for ninety-five percent of all Protestant believers, the highest single act they engage in as Christians is the act of "going to church." And as long as "going to church" is our highest act and our most obvious definition of our faith—and the number one image we project to the world—that is as far as the Christian faith is ever going to travel!)

Go back to Galilee. Look at your Lord. Think about Him. Do any of those meetings I have just mentioned match what Jesus Christ was after? Are those sermons you hear (do you really hear them?)

the thing Jesus had in mind when He came to earth? *Is that church service what Jesus Christ came to earth to establish?* In heaven, before the incarnation, did He dream that one day the church would be on earth and it would gather as do Catholics? No? Eastern Orthodox? Doesn't fit, does it? Well, neither does the Protestant church service.

None match our Lord. None project Him, and none project your faith in Him. Did Jesus Christ die in order for us our present-day church service? You know it is not true.

The Lord would have never thought up the Protestant church service. Never. It flies in the face of all that He is or that He purposed. You know there is nothing in the life of Jesus Christ—not one shred of a moment of His life—that indicates He wanted His followers to gather in that way! Nor did He want *that* kind of definition of His faith projected to the world. Yet we have defined Christ to a world with those very meetings. Meetings as unappealing as the Catholic meeting, a Greek Orthodox meeting, or any other kind of religious gathering.

All religious ritual, repeated over and over, no matter how ornate, or how logical, or how philosophically it is defended . . . *kills.*

The world's image of our Lord, His work and His purpose are shouted to the world every time we go into a church building, sit down and stare blankly ahead.

What if this gosh-awful image of our faith had never happened? What if the Protestant church service had never happened? What if first-century meetings had survived? Do you really think you could peddle something like today's Protestant church off on God's people?

Consider this: What if the Christian faith had

remained lay-led, if we had always met in homes, if our meetings had been organic, spontaneous and varied—and different in different places all over the world. If the passionate love and care for one another were beheld by all men, *what would be the world's view of "Christian" today?* Its view of us would be radically different from how it views us right now. Our meetings define us!

Let's get rid of this pernicious way of defining our faith. We must redefine our faith by utterly changing the way churches are born and how they arrive at the way they meet! Let us change for our own sake! (Let's stop the pain!) Let us change for the sake of the world because the world really does not know who we Christians are.

That is our fault. We propagandize this distorted view of the Christian faith every time we open the door to a church building. A heathen thinks he will have to go to one of those things if he gets saved. Consequently, he does not want to get saved. (I am not sure I blame him.)

If we met in homes, experienced "community"—whatever that is—had an unending variety of ways to gather, and were a lay-led movement . . . you could never sell the present Sunday church service to anyone! We would gag at the thought!

"Going to church" is a tragic, *pitiful* way to define our Lord and our faith. And yet it stands forever fixed and never challenged, despite its all-destructive nature.

We Christians have spent well over 400 years concentrating on our theology. We have believed that if we got our theology straight and got our people believing proper theology, that one accomplishment would vanquish all the demons of unscripturality and theological error and therein cure all the church's ills.

In the meantime, we utterly overlooked a problem every bit as destructive as poor theology; we overlooked the tragedy of the practice of the way we Christians meet!

Our practices are pitiful! And speaking of unscriptural . . .

The Sunday church service is *omnipresent*, that is, it is practiced in exactly the same way, be it in a church building on Main Street, or in the jungles of Africa, or the igloos of Greenland!

This ritual is also *omnipotent* in its power to render useless all else we do. Its destructive power is incalculable, a vast black hole that vacuums away all else. Every adaptation or improvement we think up for a cure to our ills overlooks and never touches the sermon, never addresses the problem of a *dead church service* or *mute* laymen. Nor does it ever address the need of returning the Christian faith to (1) itinerant church planters and (2) functioning laymen—functioning in the meeting.

Either the Sunday-go-to-church-sit-in-pew-listen-to-sermon-get-up-go-home practice is eliminated, or all else we have done, are doing, or will ever do will be castrated by the deadly powers of that practice.

In the place of Sunday church must come a revolution as great as any this world has ever witnessed . . . the lay-led discovery of local culture-fitting, native, spontaneous and organic ways of gathering around the Lord Jesus Christ.

If there were a truly native way Christians in inland China were meeting, an American would think their ways of meeting a *little* unusual. Take one of those Chinese, in an obscure village in China, and fly him over here to attend a truly organic, native expression of the ekklesia here in our country, and he would think the different kinds of meetings we had were a little odd.

That is the way things are supposed to be!

Unfortunately, we Americans and British have never allowed the *birth* of an organic expression of the church, *anywhere*. Consequently, Chinese who live in inland China, Zulus in Africa and Americans in Texas all meet the same way. *This must end.* We have all got to go back to square one and find—for ourselves—the way the church spontaneously meets in each of our different societies and cultures.

That is Point One of this book. Point Two is how to get started on this quest.

Let us not come up with another tack-on or adaptation. Either let things remain just as they are

OR

Let us foment a radical revolution of the highest order!

Listen and you will hear a distant drummer. Look up and you will see a cloud the size of a man's hand. Sniff the air and you will smell the first scent of a revolution brewing. And look around you. What do you see? Bored, restless and hungry people.

Find that distant drum!

Now, one last look at how *not* to have church. After that, the practical.

"During the first century had someone attempted to introduce our present-day way of meeting on Sunday morning, he would have been thought mad."

15

Just Because the Sunday Morning Church Service Has Been Around For 500 Years Is That the Way God Ordained Meetings To Be?

Let us look at the origin of this 500-year-old Sunday morning assembly of boredom and death.

I have a theory: Some 500,000,000 Protestants go to church on Sunday morning enduring the church service which John Calvin invented because they unconsciously believe it is God's way of punishing them for their sins! Go to church, endure its agonies, and God calls it even! You have been properly punished and *earned* forgiveness by doing penance! You suffered through a Sunday church service!

That brings us to John Calvin. John Calvin of Geneva invented the Sunday morning church service. Do you know who he is? If you *think* you know, you are in for a shock!

There is a truism about history. If you change history, you are a hero. Calvin is a hero. He fathered many denominations.

The government-financed church of Scotland came about by way of Calvin. And in Europe if anyone tells you, "I belong to the *Reform* church," he is telling you he goes to the church founded by John Calvin. In North America they are called Presbyterians.

Calvin is praised as having one of the most titanic minds in human history. His lectures, known to the world as "Calvin's Institutes" are (excuse the pun) an institution of the Protestant faith. These lectures, when bound together as books—with small print—are about a yard thick. It takes years to read them. Has any man in history ever had so many of his thoughts, words, ideas, philosophies and theologies preserved? Possibly not.

There *are* nice stories told about the man among all Reform churches and seminaries. (Tread softly, you who would so much as raise an eyebrow in his direction.)

I raise an eyebrow.

I do not like the fact that 500,000,000 of us have to endure the abysmal misery of the Sunday ritual he invented. I personally believe that the Sunday morning ritual should be done away with. (I realize in saying that, that if that ritual *were* done away with, Protestant Christianity would have to reinvent itself. *That* is not a bad idea!)

I do not like laymen being silenced. I do not like to sit for an eternal hour in an auditorium when I could be home, sitting in front of my Kenmore washer watching it go into spin dry! Believe me, the second is a lot more fun than the first.

WHAT KIND OF MAN INVENTED THE SUNDAY CHURCH SERVICE?

Let us return to Geneva, Switzerland, circa 1545 A.D. and find out.

Geneva was *ruled* with an iron fist by seventeen men. They were referred to as the Consistory Committee. (Yep, everybody was supposed to live a life *consistent* with how they were told to live.) Five of these men were pastors; twelve were church elders. Those seventeen men ruled Geneva. Calvin ruled the seventeen.*

It was one of the most despotic governments in the history of the western world. It was a police state. *All* the lives of all the people were under rule, scrutiny and surveillance. Invasion of privacy was the order of the day.

It seems that ministers believe our call is to make people sin as little as possible. Here is a man who lived by this idea. A city was forced to live that way, too.

A few rules?**

Adultery: Death by burning at the stake.

Witchcraft: Ditto.

Missing Church Service Frequently: Death by being burned alive.

Heresy: Death by being burned alive. Heresy defined: *Anyone who dared disagree with Calvin's theology.*

(I think we are seeing a pattern develop here.)

Everybody got off the first time. Nobody got off the third time. Anyone could be brought before the Consistory. Suspicion was tantamount to guilt. You could be imprisoned at will.

You were told what kind of clothes to wear. Dress was by caste (that is, by your standing in society). Calvin believed that all things were predestined by God, including your place in society. Pity the poor soul who tried to break out of his caste—he was in rebellion against divine sovereignty.

Children had to be named after Bible characters.

---

* Will Durant, The Reformation. *pp. 472-484 (Simon & Schuster, New York 1957.)*

** *People with weak hearts should not read beyond this.*

A gentleman refused and named his child something else—he went to jail for four days.

No relics, church bells, candles; no rouge or "powdering," no jewelry, no immodest dress. (Guess who decided what was and wasn't!) No sorcery, cards, drunkenness, lace, hunting. No books that were not religious or moral in nature. No dancing. No singing of non-Christian songs. No statues.

If a child struck his parents, he was beheaded.

But, as always, sex was the big no-no. Any sex outside of marriage and you were drowned. Pregnant outside of wedlock, the same. The man was drowned, too. You do not believe? Calvin's stepson was caught and drowned. His daughter-in-law was caught and drowned; so were the other two people involved.

Tenderhearted soul, this Calvin.

Fourteen women accused of witchcraft were burned alive.

Reasoning behind such cruel punishment? I quote Calvin:

> "When the Catholics are so harsh and violent in their defense of their *superstitions*, are not Christ's magistrates shamed to do less in defense of the truth."

I think Jesus would have been burned alive in Geneva!

But what of the man Calvin? Well, he called those who disagreed with him: idiots, riffraff, pigs, asses, stinking beasts, and dogs.

This is the man who invented the Sunday church service! I am not fond of the thought that when I am sitting in "church" on Sunday morning, I am following a ritual invented by a man with so congenial an attitude toward others.

Someone put a placard in Calvin's pulpit accusing

him of hypocrisy. Calvin, as he frequently did, went into a blind rage. He could not tolerate the slightest disagreement with his views. Well, there was a suspect. No evidence, though. Arrested, the man was brutally tortured for one month. Finally he confessed—who would not? They then drove wooden spikes through his feet and forthwith chopped his head off.

Now to the point. If you lived in Geneva, you had to go to church. When you did, you sang two songs, heard a prayer, sang two more songs, heard a prayer, gave an offering, and then sang another song. If you went where Calvin spoke—St. Peter's—he spoke from one to three hours. Or you could try any of the other dozen Calvinist churches. All had the same service. Calvin genuinely believed that people enjoyed doing the aforementioned and enjoyed his sermons.

Well, dear brother Calvin, now that you are safely dead, may I share with you the truth: We didn't like your long lectures nor your order of services then; we don't now. You killed functioning. You created a silent laity.

Why have I done what I have done in this chapter to poor brother Calvin? There is a very *good reason.* Men today try every which way to justify Calvin's church service ritual. All are truly weak defenses. So men fall back on this one: Perhaps God inspired Calvin to come up with this service.

Would God have inspired John Calvin to cause 500,000,000 Protestant Christians to meet this way every Sunday morning? I do not know. But by your line of reasoning, sir, God also inspired Calvin's Geneva!

I rest my case.

Calvin, some of us are through with your church

service. There are better ways than this to gather together. Night and day have more in common than does the way we meet today versus the *ways* we could meet today. There is no comparison.

Isn't 450 years long enough?

Let's now see how to return to first principles.

"'Unless it is in a building, with a pulpit, pews, pastor, steeple, and sermon, it is not church,' is today's view of what is and is not 'church.'
"Well, if believers of the first century ever saw our version of church they would declare that ***this*** *is not church."*

16

Returning to the Home Is But a Starting Place

Why meet in a home?

Because all the churches mentioned in the New Testament met in homes. The one exception was the church in Jerusalem which also had access to the Jewish temple. All other ekklesia of the first century met in homes.

There are an estimated 100,000 home churches in China, 8,000 in South America, approximately 200

**In Russia, during the reign of communism, Christians met wherever they could. Of course, this included the home, but this did not come about because of a commitment to the home church nor was there any vision whatsoever of church life. Meeting in homes was solely a matter of necessity. Even in the home, the pastoral reign and the Protestant ritual dominated. When persecution ended, the meeting in houses vanished and the churches returned to the traditional way of meeting i.e. church buildings, pews, pastors and the John-Calvin-invented Sunday morning ritual.*

That is not true in China. A good number of those churches which meet in homes will continue to meet in homes even when persecution disappears because many of the Christians in China are committed to practices that are not part of present-day traditional practices of Christianity. May their tribe increase!

in Australia and at least 70 in New Zealand. Oddly enough, almost no home churches exist in the United States. Today there are thousands upon thousands of home gatherings, but the purpose is simply to fellowship with one another or to do Bible study. This is not the church. Furthermore, the titanic commitment to church life is totally absent.*

Are there any more destructive forces at work in all Christendom than the church building, the sermon, the pew? Meeting in homes does not solve all problems, and may solve none at all, but it is a large step *toward* a beginning.

Theologians have a philosophy to justify the reason all pews face the pulpit! Can you believe that?

(They have a philosophy for everything they do to us. The more unscriptural, the more *profound* the philosophy.) This particular philosophy is transparently erroneous, and, in general, is odorous. But you need to hear it. Theologians will state this indefensible idea with such spiritual profundity, it may very well intimidate you:

"We all face toward the Word of God to show our reverence for Scripture and our agreement with it."

All right, fellas, here is a philosophical reply to your philosophy about pews:

"If we all face toward the pulpit, we acknowledge that the clergy and the sermon are everything, that the clergy functions and we do not, and that the clergy tells us what to do, controls our worship, our fellowship and our very lives! We are only fringe accessories, spare parts of a meeting. We are an audience called in, making it possible for the clergy to perform!!

"We should not all face forward. From a philosophical view—if your philosophy demands a philosophical response—then we should face one another. We are, after all, the body of Christ. In so doing, we show our care and our love for one another and acknowledge the centrality of the Christ who dwells within us. We also function and participate in all meetings. When we do, we are fulfilling our role of functioning while facing each other, not the clergy. By facing one another we *can* function. In no other direction can we do this. While facing all the saints, we declare that the church belongs to God and to the redeemed, not to *anyone* else. Especially is the ownership of the church *not* the clergy's. Our central focus is not where it has been for 500 years, *on the clergy*. Our focus is Christ and one another; our eyes are on one another.

"By looking at one another we demonstrate that any message we might hear is only *part* of church life. The clergy's sermon is not the all nor the center, nor is anything else we do. Only Christ is. And when we gather, our worship of Him is not under the absolute control of one man, or *any* ritual.

"We face one another because we are all one body."

Personally, I think very poorly of any and all church practices justified by a philosophy. The idea is to use a profound philosophical statement to justify our wholly unbiblical practices. Watch out for profound statements which *preserve* the status quo.

The fact lies here: The pew is one of the two or three most destructive elements at work in all Christendom. Let us begin our revolt by taking dead aim at the pew and the direction it faces.

THE VIEW FROM THE PLATFORM

Ministers may not understand how this could be so monumentally important . . . but just look where the minister is sitting. Now he has one very spectacular view!

The minister is in front, up on a raised platform, looking *down.* (*Down* on *you.*) What does he see?

He sees a thousand well-scrubbed faces and beautifully dressed bodies. But more! He sees 2,000 eyes glued on *him.*

Sure! Why not pews! ? All of them facing me! An actor would kill for a role like that!

The average minister will *never* concede to this revolution. He is too central to the production . . . all floodlights shine on him. And, generally speaking, he is bereft of all understanding of church life.

Now, let's step down off the platform, go into the audience, and get a look at what *you* are seeing.

Just exactly what are you seeing, anyway? You sit in that pew for an hour, with *nothing* to do but look at the back of someone's *neck.* That is all you see! For one hour! You sit. You are silent. You stare at the back of a head!!

That is Christianity? This is why Christ died for you?

When the Scripture says, "Christ loved the ekklesia and died for her" . . . is this what God had in mind as the ultimate for the redeemed!? Examining the back of someone's head, sitting through a boring ritual? Is this to be the consummation of your participation in the gathering of the body of Christ? You, inheriting the backside of a strangers neck? For1700 years no one has revolted against this. Let us revolt!!

Have you ever been in one of those awful meetings when the pastor took leave of his senses and asked if anyone present had a testimony to share in the meeting? After what seemed an agonizing hour, some dear sainted sister got up and shared. (She could not bear the silence any longer, so she sacrificed herself.)

Keep that moment in mind! She got up and actually *functioned.* She actually *participated* in a meeting! Now think back. Did the pews really allow for sharing or functioning? (No more than a hanging allows for romance.)

If the lady who stood up to share was in front of you, you could not find her. You heard only a vaguely muffled voice. If she was behind you, then you had to turn all the way around (which cannot be done in a pew) to look for her. And isn't it peculiar, when you did manage to turn around, you then had hundreds of bewildered eyes staring at you for committing the blasphemy of *not looking forward!* Anyway, you were glad when it was over.

Pews do not allow for *any* functioning. Functioning in a meeting is described in first-century literature, but none of that which is described could be done from pews . . . or in any church building configuration.

Today it is hard for any Christian to imagine a gathering in a living room so electric that it goes on for hours. One that, when someone suggests "It's past midnight, maybe we had better go home so the Johnsons can get to bed since they have to be up at 5 a.m.," everyone groans in disappointment because no one wants the meeting to end.

It happens. Yes, on this planet. But not in sanctuaries or from pews.

We will never restore church life, we will never see a truly vital ekklesia, until the *pew* is displaced. *We will function only when we can comfortably face one another.*

Oh, some churches *have* done away with the pew! They have come to realize pews are outdated! What is trendy now is *chairs!* Chairs lined up next to one another in rows, facing forward and then soldered together!! *A pseudo-pew!* Wow, what innovation! (Bad habits die slowly.)

There is a fellow out there reading this book who is saying, "Oh, you have never been to *our* church.

We have seen the *recovery of worship.* We even have a worship leader . . . and *everyone* functions."

That, sir, is simply *not* true. (You must be one of those folks sitting up on the platform!)

What our worship leaders have allowed us to do is this: Now we don't just sit, now we can stand! And raise our hands over our heads! Wow!! Thank you for such liberty! What a breakthrough! But still, sir, all we see is the back of necks! What you see from up on the platform is a wave of glory. We see mostly haircuts and perms!!

And *you,* Mr. Worship Leader, are still in *control.* Of *everything!* All things are still originating from the clergy—the top—and being passed on down to us—*the bottom.*

Furthermore, with every passing week you have to pump us harder to get your idea of glory out of us in *your* meeting. Ultimately, you will have to pump so long and so hard you will be forced to lead us beyond Christian worship to *heathen frenzy* in order to get us to the peak where we were previously.

I repeat, nothing is going to cure the Sunday church service except to obliterate it.

The only way the body of Christ will ever be known and experienced is when we pursue our discovery of ekklesia for ourselves. Not by clergy control. Not by ritual. Or anything that begins at the top. Church life is to be discovered. By us. By us peasants here at the bottom.

Only when *infinite variety* is the standard will routine end. Only when we are left on our own to find, for ourselves, the way we gather . . . only when we, the believers, are wholly responsible for and totally participating in the gatherings . . . only *then* will we have a consistent *reality* in the meetings. Anything short of that, no matter how new, will eventually become routine . . . and when you are stuck in routine, no matter what it is, it becomes stale. And stale becomes boring. Nothing really new will ever happen in the house of God as long as pews exist and everyone faces the same direction.

Anything short of the community of believers will become ritual. Only when the church is a community of believers plotting *their own course* will there ever be a smashing of the present-day deadlock.

Our present church practices cannot be reformed. Not to the point that routine and ritual are overcome. To arrive at such a point, present-day church practices can only be annihilated.

What do you think? Will the churches across this planet change *that* radically? If you think so, go for it! See if you can get those pews, or chairs, rearranged.

If not, the other way to foment this revolution is to walk out. If a large number of Christians would simply walk out the doors, something brand new would have to take the place of that rut. But to be able to do this, you must be totally resolved that you will not tolerate being a mute in our present-day practices. The view of the neck must go!

You must search your own heart and see if you truly are determined never to return to what was.

If you really think *your* church—just *yours*—can change this radically, then consider this: We have only discussed *one* jugular vein. There are some others we have to go for.

There is also the church building! And the ritualistic grinding out of a sermon by one soul every Sunday. And the whole ritual which precedes that sermon. *And* . . . and . . . the present-day practice of the *pastor*. The pastor as we know him today was invented by Martin Luther. Nonetheless, he is now in the DNA of present-day Christianity. We need a revelation.

The present church must change. *Or* we must start anew, from the ground up. Or you can spend the rest of your life seeing church as a place where mutes sit for an hour each Sunday examining the backside of someone's neck.

It's your choice!

* * *

We now move beyond "meeting in a home" to "*how* to begin."

"We live in a post-Christian era, but only because Christianity has sunk into religiosity."
—Gabriel Vahanian

17

Toward an Organic Meeting and an Organic Church

Our goal?

It is pretty formidable. It is twofold: (1) to place the meetings of the ekklesia under the headship of Jesus Christ—that takes a little time; (2) in the process, to see emerge an organic way of meeting within a fellowship of believers. This means a way of meeting, a way of expressing the body of Christ, that is natural to your soil, to your culture, to your people: an indigenous church. A meeting should "fit" a people, even to the point that if an unbeliever in your own town came into one of your meetings, there would be an atmosphere that was comfortable, or at least, understandable to his culture. That is, he would not feel he had just walked through a door into some foreign land.

Getting such a reality—starting from where we are—is not easy! It takes discovery. It implies having a people who are willing to take an adventure into the unknown . . . *discovering* a way to meet.

Remember: To assist believers in discovering this organic expression of the ekklesia takes a little time.

To have meetings with *no* leaders present—successfully—takes a little time. A church that can survive without any leaders within its membership

. . . for one or two years, or more . . . takes a little time. Surviving, flourishing, in and out of meetings, that takes a little help . . . and a lot of stick-to-itiveness.

In other words, this can be a bumpy ride. The fainthearted should think twice about taking it!!

The following pages that deal with the "how" are based on my personal experience and that of others. They are passed on to you, tested under just about every circumstance imaginable. There is not a sentence here that is theory. This book is not theory. It has grown out of the crucibles of church life.

Again, dare you embark on such an adventure?

For you to go beyond this point keep the following in mind.

> In the first century the churches began as a result of the work and ministry of church planters. These men were itinerant. (They moved around. They did not stay with any ekklesia very long.) The concept of the church planter has been lost to us. So has the concept of leaving a church on its own while that church is still in its infancy. So has the idea of God's people discovering for themselves how they gather as the ekklesia.
>
> This book reintroduces all of the above concepts and practices. So, if you go beyond this page you have to ask, "Am I ready for a church planter . . . et al?"
>
> There is another book for you to read. Do not venture out until you have read a book entitled: *The Man Nobody Wants.** Its subtitle is *Thoughts About Church Planters.*

**Coming in mid-2000.*

> There is nothing in this book of any value unless there is (1) a return to itinerant church planters and (2) the practice of churches' being left to be on their own while still in their infancy.

If you cannot accept a church planter in your midst, I urge you to forget everything in this book. Short of a church planter—*from outside* the group itself—you are courting a lady whose name is Disaster. If you are willing to embrace this *long*-forgotten way and this audacious person called a church planter, you have a royal adventure awaiting you!

PART III

Starting All Over

Totally New

From the Ground Up

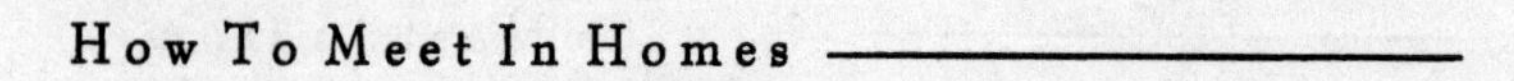

"Christ died for the church.
Paul was beaten, stoned, imprisoned, persecuted and beheaded for the church.
The version of the church they died for is not today's version of church."

18

Step One

The best way to discover how to meet is to start as a totally new people, with a church planter in your midst.

In fact, it is the only way. And that statement assumes the church planter is committed to leading this body of believers to the point they are able to meet under the headship of Jesus Christ. And *that* includes the necessity for his *leaving.*

But even under such ideal circumstances, you face formidable problems.

FUNCTIONING? WHAT IS THAT?

God's people simply do not know how to function when they get together. It is going to take a long time and a lot of patience before the people who are present with you, now gathered in someone's home, hope to carry the total burden of a meeting. Never mind that one day you "laymen" will have to carry *all* the responsibility of church life. Right now just learning to function is a steep mountain to scale.

Therefore, in the coming pages we will deal with this one singularly overriding problem: finding the solution to the problem of getting people to function.

After that, the problem of functioning *on so shallow a level that even Sunday morning church starts to look good again!*

The solution to this problem embraces both things practical and things spiritual.

WHAT, NO MINISTER?!

The first problem is the difficulty of people learning to function. The second major problem is the minister. *What is his problem?* The answer to that is easy! *Ministers simply cannot give up ministering!*

People will not function; ministers will not stop functioning! Paradoxical, is it not? Those are your first two obstacles to church life. Expect radical solutions.

Ministers also cannot stop leading. That includes not only ministers, but ministers of education, ministers of children, ministers of music (*and* worship leaders), because a rose by any other name is still a rose!

Too often there are one or two other people, along with all these ministers, who are in some type of leadership position. They cannot stop functioning, either! In the meantime, God's people have a mindset of "our place is to sit there in the pew and listen." The result? You end up with meetings in which functioning never gets off the ground.

Only the most radical of changes will break this double bind! The task of changing these two interlocking problems is Himalayan. The time needed to break this bind—even in a radical venture—is not short. Sometimes it is very long. (Would that we could have a clear slate like the Albanians had!)

Years ago, when I did not know better, I encouraged ministers in traditional churches to have meetings in which the people shared. I presented to them and their people everything necessary to have such meetings. *But it never happened.* The Lord's people would not function, and the ministers simply would not turn God's people loose. Or, perhaps, it went the other way around—the minister simply could not (either from orientation or from fear) turn a meeting over to the Lord's people without having someone present who was a recognized leader.

We have a problem. A big one. No, that is not correct: It is gigantic. Once more I offer this sincere doubt: I doubt a traditional church will ever accomplish this!

Please prove me wrong!

Dear reader, just look at a church building. The way that thing sits there and glares at you virtually precludes open, informal sharing. The thing says, "I am against it!" Again, please prove me wrong. I will be the one rejoicing the loudest.

You must add the even greater intimidation of the presence of a minister. That would intimidate an Elijah!

Sorry, but with those two strikes against you—in my judgment—you do not stand a chance to have organic church life.

Burn the building, send the preacher to Kalamazoo and maybe . . . just maybe . . . you might make it. But even then, the Lord's people seem to be locked in fear, intimidated by all that is "church." You need only watch how the Lord's people act when they, the laymen, know they will have to be in charge of a Lord's Supper and, terror of terrors, there will be no minister present.

No, seventeen hundred years of silence is now in our bloodstream.

If this is true, why is it true? I think the answer is very simple.

THE MAN NOBODY WANTS

Dear brothers and sisters, you need to passionately believe in the body of Christ with all your heart, soul, mind and strength.

In the face of all these problems which will come, you must passionately believe that the Lord can become head of the meetings. Laymen must be trusted, utterly trusted.

(Laymen have to believe, too. Totally!)

That brings us to the hard part. Who is the man who will be leading the Lord's people toward these wonderful matters of open meetings, a pastorless church, a church without an auditorium, laymen in charge of everything, meetings under the headship of Christ?

He has to be consumed with the headship of Christ. He has to burn for the ekklesia. He has to believe in laymen more than he believes in anything else on this earth.

He has to be a man consumed! He has to believe God's people will function. He has to believe that, with a little help in the beginning, they can carry a meeting from start to finish. That they can eventually have glorious meetings. He has to believe that!

He has to believe that God's people can gather under the direct headship of Jesus Christ. He has to believe that the Lord can actually lead the meeting. That Jesus Christ is alive enough to lead His own people. He has to believe this is what God is wanting on this earth and always has wanted. He has to believe all this can be done, despite all the failures of the past. He has to stick with these beliefs, however long it takes, come hell or high water. He has to be committed to this until these things begin to happen.

And most unlikely of all, everyone will have to believe that it is God's ordained way that these things all come to pass by means of the presence and help of . . . a church planter. An *extra-local* church planter.

Everyone is committed to a return to the first-century concept of an itinerant church planter? Easy? Well, can you see the pastoral concept (which is now at the center of the stage) totally disappear? Can you see the church planter—who has been absent for 1700 years—again taking his rightful place on that stage?

Perhaps *that* is the pivotal point.

It may be that (1) without that vision, that revelation of Jesus Christ, and (2) without that revelation of His bride, and (3) without seeing that church planter on every page in the book of Acts and in every epistle—there is no way under God's heaven these things will ever come into being again!

Let me qualify that. Church life is spontaneous. Actually, church life is experienced all over America, all over the world, every day . . . in spontaneous little gatherings and home meetings. But those wonderful, brief little "ekklesia experiences" die out as quickly as they begin. Some last up to six months. A few last two years.

They all die.

The pain involved in the dying is some of the most terrible and brutal pain a Christian can ever experience.

Why does spontaneous church life die? Because no one wants the one thing that is so necessary. If we hope to have church life on this earth again, it will be with the reappearance of that one thing. Dear reader, to have the ekklesia, then *ekklesia planters* are needed. Such men were an absolute necessity in the first century. They are still a necessity today. And they will be a necessity tomorrow. This is an immutable, immovable, unchangeable, unalterable fact. It is just God's way! And He will not budge.

The commitment of that church planter has to be as great as his *call* from the Lord and his being *sent* by the Holy Spirit.

IN 2399 A.D.

History tells us of small numbers of believers who recorded their experience of meeting in this way. They left a legacy for the future generations who would come after them. Their testimony cries out, "It can be done!" Our age must leave that same legacy to future generations. At the very least we must exhibit that same testimony so that others out there in the future may get a glimpse of *how the church ought to be.*

If you pick up this book in the year 2399 A.D., know that you hold in your hand the experiences of those who gathered together under the headship of Jesus Christ back in the primitive days of that dark age of the twenty-first century! We trust we have left you that very legacy.

And now, to really get your attention as to just how different all this is, in comparison to what is going on around us . . .

"After the day of Pentecost, the believers ordained pastors, set up church buildings, told everyone to sit quietly—not to talk—and then preached sermons every Sunday for the next 100 years. And everyone loved this. They got so excited about this way of being the church that they swept the entire Roman empire."

19

Step Two and Three

You are about twelve to twenty-five people who are setting out on the adventure of your lives. You are going to begin by meeting together in a home. That home is all you have. If the number is more than twenty, fine.

We assume the presence of a genuine church planter among you. We assume that, from the very first day, it is understood by all that he will one day leave the church to gather on its own.

Please note that no attempt is made to meet without the help of the church planter during the earliest days. No experimentation. No "going it alone." You need that church planter. When you start out, please understand you are at least six months from "trying it on your own!"

(Go back and take a close look at the birth of all those Gentile churches. The church planter is at the center of everything going on. This is true from *day one* until *departure day!)*

YOUR VERY FIRST GET-TOGETHERS

Never try to have an actual "church meeting," not at the outset. It will fail so miserably, no one will really believe it is possible to have a truly wonderful meeting with no leadership present! You have to begin somewhere else. Do not try a meeting per se!

It would be impossible to relate to you how many groups get a vague idea about "meeting" and try to have their own. If you do that, please never use my name. I have heard of disasters; I have *seen* even worse ones with my own eyes. I *never* want to be in such meetings. Sitting in a living room does not make church life! And if you fill that room with the world's greatest theologians and Bible scholars or *only* new converts . . . it will still be a disaster. No exceptions.

First you need ministry. You need help. Lots of it. That fact is written into the laws of God. You cannot change the immutable.

Later you need to be abandoned!

So what do you do?

You begin by dropping things you have and acquiring things you do not have.

HOW NOT TO DO IT

Let me share my first-time experience at meeting. To encourage you, *it was awful.* It happened in my hometown, Tyler, Texas. A group of about fifteen of us decided we were going to start meeting in a living room. We were going to meet under the headship of Jesus Christ.

Instead we launched a comedy.

To start, we met at eleven o'clock on Sunday morning! That alone will kill a herd of elephants. Next, we all came in suits and ties. Ugh!! What happened? We sat down and stared at one another. Every time a woman came into the living room, all the men—being southern gentlemen—stood up! (Standing up when a lady entered the room was a custom in that day. Check your ancient archives.)

And no one just walked into the house. No! When anyone got to the front door, they rang the doorbell!

We all whispered and tip-toed. Silence was never so deadly. Finally, some poor soul meekly said, "Can we sing . . ."

What followed would best be forgotten! Shucks, we could not sing *anything*. The sharing was worse. Abysmal, awful and embarrassing. No, it was worse than that! Most of what we did for that hour or two was sheer agony. It was also typical of what happens to any group of Christians who try to move in this direction. (Need I tell you, we had no outside help. I doubt that at that moment there was a living soul on the North American continent who could have helped us, anyway. Throw in South America for good measure.)

I wish I could tell you that this was the only experience of disaster ever experienced by a group of Christians trying to meet together. I cannot.

Yes, to meet as a body of believers is a high goal—as high as the heart of God. But the way of getting there seems to be incredibly elusive. Actually, it is next to impossible to find.

So, how do you begin? *I recommend the following.* No, I *strongly* recommend the following. No, I *urge* you to begin this way. No, I *beg* you.

STEP THREE

We will imagine there are twenty of you. (*That* is a very large number. Realistically, even in a large city, it would probably be hard to find fifteen people willing to dare this adventure (unless, of course, there was some other agenda *also* present). Most groups begin with no more than eight or ten.

At the very outset all of you need to realize, and agree, that you will come together every week for a minimum of six months, *no* matter how bad, no matter how hopeless things get. You must be committed to one another *at least that* much. In America—three years would be wiser. Albania—only six months, maybe only four. In Albania, you might even see it happen like it did in Philippi, in only three weeks!

Meet for a minimum of eight to ten weeks, *doing nothing but eating together!* Nothing. Do not dare sing. Avoid prayer! (All right, pray over the food!) That is a pretty radical recommendation, I realize. But the roots of our religiosity go so deep it demands such a radical approach.

Those ten weeks will be an eye opener! You will discover that half the people you meet with are strange if not psychotic. Shucks, why lie to you. They are out-and-out crazy. The other half . . . the second half makes the first half look normal.

During this time, get to know one another. *Informally*, get to know one another. *That comes before all else.*

Eat together once or twice a week. Take your time to get to know each other. Be patient. (We Americans want everything fast. We want it now! And, of course, bigger and better. *Lay it down, brother.)*

You who are getting together soon learn that you are now dealing with one of the most imponderable of all equations: *fallen* human nature. And you are about to attempt the impossible: to some way crawl over that fallen nature in order to reach the realm of things spiritual.

A strong recommendation: Read the first chapter of Dietrich Bonhoeffer's *Life Together*. That should open some eyes.

As noted, there must be a clarity of purpose which—with the Lord's grace present in great *abundance*—can weather fire, famine or flood.

After five or ten weeks—or six months or a year if necessary—you probably have come to know one another *fairly* well. And despite that fact, let us hope you are still together anyway. But be warned: You still know one another on *a very superficial plane!* Trust me, the worst discoveries about one another are yet to come!

I could easily offer you several hundred signatures of saints I know who would tell you, *"Gene was being kind!"*

What is the next step:

Write or call SeedSowers for an audio message from Gene Edwards entitled:

"What Next?"

The Chronicles Heaven *(Edwards)*

The Beginning 8.99
The Escape 8.99
The Birth 8.99
The Triumph 8.99
The Return 8.99

The Collected works of T. Austin-Sparks

The Centrality of Jesus Christ 19.95
The House of God 29.95
Ministry 29.95
Service 19.95
Spiritual Foundations 29.95
The Things of the Spirit 10.95
Prayer 14.95
The On-High Calling 10.95
Rivers of Living Water 8.95
The Power of His Resurrection 8.95

Comfort and healing

A Tale of Three Kings (*Edwards*) 8.99
The Prisoner in the Third Cell (*Edwards*) 5.99
Letters to a Devastated Christian (*Edwards*) 5.95
Exquisite Agony *(Edwards)* 8.95
Dear Lillian (*Edwards*) 5.95

Other books on church life

Climb the Highest Mountain (*Edwards*) 9.95
The Torch of the Testimony (*Kennedy*) 14.95
The Passing of the Torch (*Chen*) 9.95
Going to Church in the First Century (*Banks*) 5.95
When the Church was Young (*Loosley*) 8.95
Church Unity *(Litzman, Nee, Edwards)* 10.95
Let's Return to Christian Unity *(Kurosaki)* 10.95

Christian Living

The Autobiography of Jeanne Guyon 19.95
Final Steps in Christian Maturity (*Guyon*) 12.95
Turkeys and Eagles *(Lord)* 8.95
The Life of Jeanne Guyon *(T.C. Upham)* 17.95
The Ultimate Intention (*Fromke*) 10.00
Unto Full Stature (*Fromke*) 10.00
All and Only (*Kilpatrick*) 7.95
Adoration (*Kilpatrick*) 8.95
Bone of His Bone (*Huegel*) *modernized* 8.95
Rethinking the Wineskin *(Viola)* 8.95
Who is Your Covering? *(Viola)* 6.95
You Can Witness with Confidence *(Rinker)* 14.95

*Prices subject to change

Books you might like to read.

Radical books for radical readers

Beyond Radical

A simple, historical introduction into how we got all of our present-day Christian practices.

You will be thunderstruck to discover that there is really nothing we are doing today in our church practice that came directly out of man's determination to be scriptural. Virtually everything we do came into being sometime during church history, after the New Testament. We have spent the rest of our time trying to bend the Scripture to justify the practice.

When the Church was Led only by Laymen

The word *elder* appears in the New Testament seventeen times, the word *pastor* appears only once (and nobody knows what that word had reference to, because there is no place in the first-century story in which he is clearly seen.)

But there are over one hundred and thirty references from the day of Pentecost forward that refer to either "brothers" or "brothers and the sisters" (Greek: *Adolphus*). *These* were the people who were leading the church. There are only two major players, from a human viewpoint, upon the first-century stage. They are the church planters and God's people - the brothers and sisters. Everything else is a footnote.

Books which show what the Christian faith was like "First-Century Style"

Revolution, the Story of the Early Church

The Silas Diary

The Titus Diary

The Timothy Diary

The Priscilla Diary

The Gaius Diary

The Story! Perhaps the best way we will ever understand what it was like from the day of Pentecost in 30 A.D. until the close of the first-century is simply to know the story. Allow yourself to be treated to, and enthralled by that story. (Warning: Knowing the story will change your life forever.) You will find that story in every detail, with nothing missing, in these *six* books.

New Testament

The Story of My Life as told by Jesus Christ

Matthew, Mark, Luke and John combined into one complete gospel written in first-person singular.

Acts in First-Person

Beginning with Acts 1, Peter tells the story of Acts through chapter 11. Then Barnabas, speaking in first person, tells the story of Acts from chapter 13 to chapter 15. You then hear Silas, Timothy and Luke continue the story all the way through, ending with chapter 28.

Books which show you how to experience Christ

The following books serve as an introduction to the deeper christian life:

Living by the Highest Life
The Secret to the Christian Life
The Inward Journey

Books that heal

Here are books that have been used all over the world, and in many languages, to heal Christians from the deep, deep pains they experiences as they go through life. Some were written for Christians who have been damaged by their churches and damaged by other Christians. Others are books which help you understand the ways of God as they are know working in your life. All of these books are known and loved around the world.

A Tale of Three Kings

A study in brokenness based on the story of Saul, David and Absalom.

The Prisoner in the Third Cell

A study in the mysteries of God's ways, especially when He works contrary to all your understanding and expectations of Him.

Exquisite Agony

Pain suffered by a Christian at the hands of another believer is one of the most destructive experiences one will ever know, let this book start the healing.

Letters to a Devastated Christian

This book explores different techniques practiced by Christian groups who demand extreme submission and passivity from their members. It faces the difficult task of dealing with bitterness and resentment and rebuilding of faith and trust.